Shattered PROMISES

J. L. BOOTH

Copyright

Editing by KP Editing
Formatting & Cover Design by KP Designs
- www.kpdesignshop.com
Published by Kingston Publishing Company
- www.kingstonpublishing.com

Table of Contents

Dedication

For Josh

Thank you for always pushing me to write even when I didn't want to and for always encouraging me when I didn't believe in myself.

"Hearts get infiltrated. Promises get broken. Rules get shattered. Love gets ugly."

- Colleen Hoover

1

I stared into the sea of people and watched as they swayed their hips and grinded their asses to the beat of the music. Unsure of what I'm even doing here, I take a sip of my drink and look around trying to find Halle. I can't believe I let her talk me into coming out tonight. She knows I don't party or go to clubs, but she insisted on getting me out of the house for once. Literally would not leave me alone until I said yes.

"Come on Bells, it will be fun," she whined.

"No. I have so much work to do. I can't."

"All you ever do is work. You have to get out every now and then. How do you expect to meet a guy if you are always locked up in this house?"

"I don't have time for guys, Halle. You know that."

"The only time you ever leave this house is when you go to work or the gym. You don't even go shopping anymore. It's sad. And I'm worried about you."

"You don't have to worry. The new CEO is making everyone work extra hard these days."

"What's his deal anyway?" she asks, as she browses through my closet trying to find an outfit for me to wear tonight.

"I have no idea. I still haven't met him."

"It's been, what, six months since he took over the place?"

"Something like that."

"And we haven't met him yet?"

"No. No one has. You know he has never even been to the office." We work for a very prestigious law firm, Taylor, Johnson, and now Thayer. It was just Taylor and Johnson Law Firm but when Mr. Thayer took over as CEO his name got added to the sign since he is supposed to be a practicing lawyer. Doesn't seem like he does much work if he hasn't even been in the building.

I was jolted out of my thoughts when a girl who is wasted as fuck bumped into me and spilled her drink on my shoes. "OMG. I am so sorry." She slurred her words, further proving just how drunk she is. She can't be more than 21. Her blonde hair is a mess, and her mascara has started to run from the sweat she was working up from dancing.

I sat my drink on the bar and headed for the bathroom. Luckily, my shoes weren't ruined but my feet were starting to become sticky from whatever sweet drink she had in her glass. I'm more of a whiskey girl but, to each their own. Thankfully, the line to the bathroom wasn't very long and I was able to clean my feet rather quickly. I cleaned and dried my shoes the best I could, but they didn't feel the same. I was annoyed and ready to go. I left the bathroom in haste to find Halle.

I walked every inch of the club and couldn't find her anywhere. The sea of bodies wasn't making it very easy for me. Every time I walked by a guy that wasn't with a girl already, they would try to grab me for a dance. I politely rejected them and most of them were okay with letting me walk away. There were a couple of guys that were a little more persistent but eventually got bored and let me go. That is until I bumped into a brute of a man. He looked like he spent too much time in the gym. His muscles are protruding out of his shirt that was much too small for him and not in a sexy way either.

"Hey there darling. You looking for a dance?"

"No thanks," I said, as I tried to scoot past him.

"How about just one dance?"

"No thanks. I'm looking for my friend."

"Just one dance and I'm sure your friend will find you."

"No," I said more sternly.

"A girl in a club dressed like that is only looking for one thing darling. And I just might be what you're looking for."

"Yeah? And what exactly would that be?" I snapped while clenching my fist.

"You know, a fun time."

"I'll pass," I said as I tried to pass by him once more. He grabs my arm and pulls me against his body. "Let go of me," I snapped.

"I think you need to let her go. Now." A man said from behind me.

"Who are you?" The big guy asked.

"I will be your worst fucking nightmare if you don't let her go right fucking now."

"You?" The big guy laughed. "You are half the size of me. What do you think you could actually do to me?" The big guy pulled me in tighter ignoring whoever was behind me.

"Last warning mother fucker." The guy behind me said.

The big guy holding me pushed me behind him but kept a hold of my arm to make sure I didn't run off. He took a step closer to the man taking up for me. He was blocking my view so I still couldn't see who he was. "Or what?" he asked through clenched teeth. Without a word the man punched the big guy and he instantly fell to the side and hit the floor. He was out cold. Shocked, I looked at the big guy on the floor and then back at my savior.

I was shocked to see who had saved me. He was tall, maybe a little over six feet. His brown hair was messed up, but on purpose. He was wearing black dress pants and his white button up shirt was unbuttoned showing a peak of his chest. The sleeves were rolled up a little showing just enough of his arms to let me know he is covered in tattoos. I could see the muscles relax and contract as he held out a hand for me. He was the most beautiful man I had ever seen. I took his hand, and he pulled me into him and put his arm around my shoulders. "Let's get you out of here."

I didn't protest. This is the last place I wanted to come tonight and it is definitely the last place I want to be when that beast of a man wakes up. I couldn't help the anxiety that was filling my body now that the adrenaline was wearing off. I couldn't believe that just happened to me. You hear stories all the time about men asserting dominance over women leading to rape and things like that, but no one ever thinks those things will really happen to them. I was so glad to have this stranger there to help me. This night would have probably been so much worse if he hadn't been there.

As soon as we stepped out of the club doors a black SUV pulled up in front of us. The man helped me into the truck and then walked around to the other side to let himself in. The warmth of his hand was keeping me steady and safe. As soon as he let go, I was scared, and my entire body started shaking. Finally, the tears started falling. I looked out the window so whoever this man was wouldn't see.

"Are you cold?" he asked.

"No," I said wiping away the tears as discreetly as possible.

"Your whole body is shaking."

"It isn't from being cold," I said, as I wrapped my arms around myself.

"Come here," he said, as he scooted closer to me. He wrapped his arm around me and tucked my head into the crease of his neck. "It'll be okay. That guy will never hurt you. I promise."

"I know," I said with a cry, and with that he grabbed my chin and forced me to look at him.

"I know we don't know each other but I'm not letting you spend the night alone. I'm taking you back to my place."

Okay was all I could say. I don't know why I am willingly letting this man take me to his home. I'm not even sure why I let him help me into his car. But one thing I know for sure is that I feel one hundred percent safe in his arms. No man has ever made me feel so safe. I have had boyfriends before, and no one compares to the way he makes me feel. I laid my head back on his shoulder as he gently rubbed his fingers up and down my bare arm.

I decided that I don't need to know his name or his life story. All I needed to know was that at least, for just one night, I was safe. And more than anything I hoped he would allow me to sleep wrapped up in his arms.

2

The drive back to his place wasn't that far from the club. The SUV stopped in front of a tall building; one I knew well. It is the only building in town to house the rich and richer. Only millionaires live here. The nerves in the pit of my stomach were causing me to shake again. I have never been in the building. I have always been curious but even though I make pretty good money as a lawyer, I don't make nearly enough to live in a place like this.

The guy got out and came around to open my door. He held out his hand to help me out of the SUV. I started to pull away once I was out, but he gripped on tight. He wasn't letting me go. Still no alarm bells were going off as I let him lead me to his home. For all I knew this man could be leading me to my death and here I am letting the nameless man do so without a single fight.

He said hello to the door man and handed him a one-hundred-dollar bill for a tip before entering the building. The door man tipped his hat to me and gave me an innocent smile. I bet he wasn't far from being rich himself if he always gets tipped like that. We entered the elevator, and I watched as he picked the button for whatever floor we were going to. I was expecting him to press any one of the numbers but instead he pressed the one that read PH. Penthouse, I assumed. This meant he had the largest home on the top floor apart from everyone else. I am sure that everyone else had huge condos too, but no one would match the size of his home.

I was excited to see what a penthouse looked like since I have never, or would never, get the chance to see one again. When the door opened, mentally, my jaw hit the floor. Everything was dark gray and black. It was clean and sleek looking. I expected everything to be white and gold for some reason. I was not expecting this. I absolutely fell in love at first sight of the place. Black is my favorite color even though most people argue that black isn't a color. We were only standing in the foyer, but it was all I needed to see to know I would never want to leave this place.

"Grand tour?" he asked, pulling me alongside him while still holding my hand.

"Sure," I said with a smile.

He led me through the foyer that led into what I would assume to be a mudroom of some sort, but this was too fancy for me to tell. "If you don't mind, I don't allow anyone to wear shoes beyond this point. I do have some slippers if you would like. The floor can sometimes be cold."

"Sure," I said, completely okay with removing my shoes. If I lived here, I wouldn't let anyone wear their shoes in my home either. I was shocked when he reached down to help remove my shoes and add the slippers. His touch on the back of my leg sent a sensation shooting through my body.

Standing back up, he took my hand once more, "This way." He led me down a short hallway that opened into a kitchen that any true chef could appreciate.

"Wow," I said, completely enthralled by the dark spacious room. It had every appliance one could think of. It had a double oven with an eight-burner stovetop. The refrigerator was one of those sub-zero fridges that was built perfectly into the wall to match the cabinets. The cabinets were all dark, of course, and the light gray granite countertops were a great contrast to the room. It felt so warm and inviting. I wanted nothing more than to start baking something right away.

"I take it you like the kitchen?"

"I mean who wouldn't?"

"It is a great kitchen. Too bad it has never been used."

"Never?" I asked in shock.

"I don't have much time for cooking. Plus, I'm not that great of a cook."

"I would take lessons to learn if I didn't know how to cook if this was my kitchen."

"So does that mean you know how to cook?"

"Some. I like to bake more though."

"Sweets? I'm not that into sweets."

"Is that because you are trying to maintain the perfect body or because you don't like sweets?"

"You think I have a perfect body?" he asked with a smile.

"Any man or woman with eyes can tell you have a perfect body. Now answer the question."

"Couple reasons actually. I do try to keep in shape."

"Obviously."

"Sweets don't make it on my regular diet."

"And the other reason?"

"When I was a kid, my father didn't allow me to eat very sweet things a lot. He said they would make us too hyper, and, in his world, a hyper kid is a bad kid. I only got sweets on birthdays, Thanksgiving, and Christmas. The rest of the year it was off limits. So, this one time when I was about thirteen, we had this elderly neighbor that was trying to rake his yard. I went over and helped him out. He ended up paying me twenty dollars. I took that twenty dollars to a little store in town and bought as much candy as that twenty dollars would buy. I took the candy home, went into my room as quietly as I could so no one would know I was there, and ate every single piece of candy. By the time I finished I was so sick, my stomach hurt, and I threw up several times. I ended up missing dinner that night and just lay in bed contemplating my life choices."

I couldn't help but laugh at his story. It was cute. "Well, you are an adult now and have the option to eat whatever you want without someone telling you that you can't have it. Besides, now you know portion control. I think you should try a dessert sometime."

"Well, since you like to bake, maybe sometimes you can make me something to try and change my mind."

"After saving me tonight I will make you whatever dessert you want."

"Shall we continue with the tour?" He led me into the living room this time. The floors were a bright wood but everything else, just like the foyer, mudroom, and kitchen, was dark grays and blacks. The couch sat in the floor instead of on top of it. It was perfectly placed in the middle of the room in front of the largest fireplace I had ever seen. There was a TV mounted on the wall above the fireplace but if you didn't know it was there you wouldn't be able to see it. That was all that was in the room. There weren't any decorations or Knick knacks of any kind. It was very clean with not a single pillow out of place. He took me down a wide hallway that had five doors down it. Two on each side and one right at the end of the hall. He pointed to the first room on the right and said, "This is my office." He opened it for a split second and let me see in. I didn't get to see much though. He then pointed to the room across the hall and said, "These two rooms on this side are guest rooms."

He then pointed at the other room on the right and said, "This is the guest bathroom." He opened the door and let me get a good look inside. The bathroom looked like it belonged in a totally different home. Everything from the ceiling, floors, walls, and everything else was pure white. And not just any white. It was bright and vibrant. It was so bright I had to squint my eyes a little to adjust to the brightness.

He pulled me along when he thought I had seen enough. He opened the last door in the hallway and said, "This is my room." His room had the same bright wood flooring as the living room, but just like every other room in this house, everything was black except the bed. The bed was a deep charcoal. Its headboard alone looked like it was comfortable enough to sleep on. The bed was fitted with black sheets and a black comforter. I could only imagine how comfortable the bed is. The room was massive. There was a sitting area off to the left. There was a couch, one chair, and a coffee table. They were facing away from the bed. I dropped his hand and walked over to the floor to ceiling windows that looked over the whole city.

"Wow," was the only response I could get out.

"Beautiful, huh?"

"So much so," I said, taking it all in. I had never seen anything so beautiful in my life. I never wanted to leave this spot.

"I will grab you something better to sleep in." He left and disappeared behind a door. When he came back out, he was holding some clothes in his hands. "I am sorry I don't have anything better. I usually don't sleep in clothes."

"It's okay. Anything is better than what I'm wearing."

"Yeah. You don't seem like the type of girl to wear something so revealing."

"I'm not. My friend Halle made me go out tonight and she made me wear this." The dress was blood red and shorter than anything I would ever put on my body. It didn't help that it was skintight and strapless.

"You can go through the door I just came out of and change."

Of course, the bathroom would be just as beautiful as every other space in this penthouse. There was a soaker tub that was so deep that if I filled it with water, I wasn't sure it wouldn't cover my head. It was also extra-long, so no knees sticking out of the water to freeze either. There were double sinks, but the counter was so long there was enough for about six sinks altogether. There was also a stand-up shower. There were no curtains, just a half wall to break up the space. The stand-up shower was massive. There are four shower heads to make sure every inch of your body is always in water. I could only dream of a place like this. I quickly changed my clothes and ran my fingers through my hair. He ended up giving me a white T-shirt and some boxers. I wasn't wearing a bra with my dress, and you can see my nipples through my shirt. It would have to do though. I couldn't be picky when he was already so hospitable.

When I walked back out to the room, he was standing at the window again but this time he was in nothing but his boxers. When he turned to face me, I swallowed hard and tried my hardest to keep my eyes on his face and not on the large package that I could clearly see in the front of his boxers.

"Do you need anything before we go to bed?" he asked. I couldn't answer. All I could do was shake my head. If I spoke there is no telling what words might come out of my mouth. He walked over to me and took my hand. He led me over to the bed, pulled the covers back and motioned for me to get in. He then walked over to the other side of the bed and crawled in himself. "Is it okay if I sleep next to you?" I nodded, giving him permission. He scooted to the middle of the bed and once he was comfortable, he grabbed me and pulled me into him. He snuggled up to my back and wrapped me in his arms. It wasn't long before both of us were off to sleep.

3

I woke up to the man kissing the back of my neck and caressing one of my breasts. A small moan escaped me as I pushed my ass against his hard cock. With my invitation, he turned me over and climbed on top of me in one swift motion. His lips crashed into mine and I instantly became wet between my legs. If I am being honest with myself, I had hoped this would happen. It has been such a long time since I have been touched by a man, I have almost forgotten what it is like.

We kissed each other with so much hunger and need. We both were clinging to the kiss as if it was our last. I think we both needed this as much as the other. He broke the kiss just long enough to pull my shirt over my head. He kissed me once more before moving down to take a rock-hard nipple into his mouth. He licked and flicked his tongue in such a way I was sure this alone would make me come. I arched my back causing him to take more of me into his mouth. He gladly obliged.

He had one hand pinching and pulling my other nipple while the other started to trail down my stomach. When he got to the waistband of the borrowed boxers I was wearing, he dipped his hand inside. His fingers found my clit in a matter of seconds. It was as if he already knew my body. He knew exactly how to touch me, how to take me right to the edge.

"I'm going to come," I plead but he pulls his hand away. I watch as he sticks his fingers into his mouth and sucks off my juices.

"Mm, you are so fucking sweet," he said with a moan. He got up on his knees and pulled down the boxers I was wearing then he removed his own. His cock sprang out of his boxers as if it was happy to finally be free. I sat up and took him in my hands. I slowly slide my hand up and down his shaft giving myself a good feel of his perfect member. I slowly put him in my mouth. I licked the precum off the tip before taking him fully. I got a lot of him in my mouth and down my throat but there was no way this man was fitting all the way. His dick was huge. I knew if we actually fucked, I would be sore tomorrow. I slowly took him in then released him fast. I did this for a few minutes and the sounds of his moans were turning me on even more. "I'm going to come too quickly if you don't stop."

I sucked him slowly once more before releasing his dick from my grasp. He pushed me back on the bed and spread my legs open. He slowly climbed on top of me and found my center with the tip of his dick. He eased it in slowly but once he was in just enough, he slammed into me causing me to scream out in delight. He was definitely having a hard time fitting inside me at first but after a few thrusts I started to open up and fit perfectly around him. With every new thrust I was getting closer to the edge. Not much longer and I would be sent right over.

"Your pussy is so wet and tight," he said. With his words I jumped right off the cliff without a para-shoot. I was coming so hard I had to dig my nails into his back. He will surely have some marks tomorrow. As I convulsed around his dick he was also sent over the edge. We both came at the same time, in sync, as if this was a normal everyday occurrence for us. It was as if his body knew mine and mine his and we knew exactly what the other was doing before we did.

He collapsed on top of me but still held his weight above my body so he wouldn't squish me. "I don't want to take my dick out of you."

"I don't want you to either," I confessed.

He kissed me softly before pulling out and lying beside me. He didn't let me go. He pulled me into him once more and snuggled into my back. Completely satisfied and content, I drifted back off to sleep.

****

When I woke up the guy wasn't in the bed next to me. I stretched and instantly regretted it. My whole body ached. But, between my legs was especially sore. As I was getting up to go to the bathroom, I spotted a note on the bedside table.

I am sorry I couldn't be here when you woke up. I have an early morning at the office. I do hope I get to see you again.
-B

There was also a phone number written on the bottom of the letter. When I went into the bathroom there were some clothes lying on the counter. I assumed they were for me. It was a pair of gray sweatpants, another white T-shirt and a gray hoodie. I slipped them on, inhaling his scent as I did so. Once I was dressed, I grabbed the note and shoved it into my purse. I pulled out my phone to check it, but it was dead.

I grabbed my shoes from the mudroom and headed towards the elevator. There was a new doorman guarding the door this time. He opened the door for me and as I walked out, he said, "There is a car waiting to take you home Miss."

"Thank you." He walked me over to the car and opened the door for me. Once I was inside the sleek black car, the driver turned to me and asked where we were headed, and I quickly gave him my address.

Once I was home, I plugged in my phone and headed straight for the shower. I turned the water on as hot as I could get it. I needed the heat to relax my muscles. Once I felt like they were worked out enough,

I scrubbed as fast as I could. I don't have much time to get ready for work. I was dreading going into the office, but at least today is Friday.

I wrapped myself in a towel and went to check if my phone was charged enough yet. When my phone sprang back to life, I had ten missed calls and several text messages from Halle. I pulled up her number and hit the green phone button.

"Where have you been?" she practically screamed at me.

"Sorry, mom. Didn't mean to worry you," I said sarcastically.

"I'm serious Bells. I was getting ready to call the cops. Where were you?"

"I was safe. I have to get ready for work or I'm going to be late. I'll tell you everything as soon as I get to the office."

"Every last detail."

"Every last detail. I promise." I hung up the phone and quickly grabbed some clothes from my closet. I wanted to stay home and lounge in B's sweatpants and hoodie all day but that isn't possible. I settled on a knee-length green pencil skirt with a thin white button up tank top. I tucked in the shirt and slipped on my nude red-bottom Louis Vuitton's. I pulled my still wet hair into a bun. I added a small amount of blush to my cheeks, some mascara, and a light pink lip gloss. I added some gold earrings, a bracelet, and a gold watch. One last look in the mirror and I was happy with my outfit.

I grabbed a cardigan that was the same color as my skirt and rushed out the door.

I am never late for work, but I guess there is always a first time for everything.

4

On the ride to work, I couldn't help but think about last night. Every moment kept playing over and over in my head. As I thought about the big burly man that could have hurt me worse than he did, I rubbed my hand on the bruise he left on my arm from grabbing me. I thought about the way the stranger saved me. The way he held my hand to keep me safe until we were safely in his bedroom. As I thought about the way he kissed me I ran my fingers along my lips still able to taste him. I became wet just thinking about the best sex I had ever had last night.

I didn't even know the man's name and I probably would never see him again, but I still couldn't get him off my mind. He plagued every thought, every cell, every second of every memory from the past twenty-four hours. Honestly, I didn't mind it. It was thrilling to have sex with a stranger. I had never done that before. I've never had a one-night stand. Every time I've ever had sex was only in a serious relationship and only after at least three months of dating each other.

When we finally arrive at the office, I am only five minutes late. Waiting for me in my office was Halle, with a very annoyed look on her face. "Good morning," I said, trying to brighten the mood.

"Don't you good morning me, at least not until you tell me why you left me at the club last night and why you weren't answering your phone. I thought you were kidnapped or something worse, like dead."

"I'm sorry. I should have told you I was leaving. But in my defense, I did look all over that place for you and *you* were nowhere to be found."

"Yeah, sorry about that. I may have hooked up with the manager of the club. The guy dicked me down good on top of his desk."

"Geez," I said as I put my stuff down on my desk.

"I told you where I was, now tell me where you were."

"Well, it's a very long story. We may not have time."

"Please, the boss isn't here, we have time."

Just as the words left her mouth, Andrew stuck his head inside of my office and said, "You haven't heard, have you?"

"Heard what?" Halle and I both asked in unison.

"The new CEO is here. He has been in his office with Myrtle all morning getting everything set up from his wants, needs, and darkest desires." Andrew is one of the paralegals that work for me and Halle. He is flamboyant and fabulous. He is literally the highlight of everyone's day and if there is tea that needs to be spilled, he's your man. Myrtle is the CEO's secretary. She is old and ancient and has been every CEO's secretary since this firm started in the early eighties.

"Holy shit," Halle said while getting up to peek out the door as if she would find him standing there.

"Have you seen him?" I asked Andrew.

"Mm hmm and girl, that man is delicious. Do you hear me? Delicious."

"Have you talked to him?" Halle asked.

"No. But I did find out from Landon, who heard it from Cathy, who swears she heard it from Myrtle, that his name is Byson."

"Like the animal?" Halle asked with a laugh.

"Also, he has a stick up his ass. All work and no play supposedly."

Myrtle stuck her head in my office and said, "Oh good, you're both here. Since the two of you are working on the biggest case in the office right now, Mr. Thayer would like a meeting with the two of you in his office."

"When?" I asked.

"Now," she said sternly as she walked away. Myrtle isn't a pleasant woman. She never smiles. She always looks like she is having the worst day of her life. To say she has resting bitch face is an understatement. She always looks like she is sucking on a sour piece of candy.

"Well, shall we?" I asked Halle. I grabbed the folder with all the information I would need on the Sampson Trade deal and headed down the hallway.

When we arrived at Mr. Thayer's office, Myrtle opened the door to let us in. Mr. Thayer was standing by the floor to ceiling window looking out over the town. A flashback from last night played in my memory of the floor to ceiling windows B had in his bedroom. Without turning to face us, he asked, "Where are we on the Sampson Trade deal?"

Halle and I exchanged a look before I answered, "Everything has been going very smoothly. We are set for signing on Monday."

"No hiccups then?" he asked, still not turning to face us.

"No, sir. Everything has been moving right along according to plan. Both parties are in agreement with the contracts. Harper Trading Company will soon be the proud new owners of Sampson Trading. For this to be a very large case everything has been very easy. The parties have both been very forthcoming and honest. There haven't been any hidden liabilities, no one has tried to sneak anything into the contracts."

"Dismissed."

"Excuse me?" I asked a little taken aback.

"The two of you are dismissed. I will set up another meeting with the two of you on Monday after the signing to see how things transpire."

Halle and I exchanged another look before leaving his office. Once we are out of ear shot from Myrtle, Halle looks at me and says, "Andrew was right, he does have a stick up his ass."

"Maybe. To me he just seemed to be distracted or deep in thought about something."

"Were we in the same meeting? The man didn't even turn to face us. How did it feel talking to his back? The man is an ass and rude. This is going to be so fucking fun working here."

"Halle, it won't be that bad. Maybe he is having a rough day. We should at least give him the benefit of the doubt. It is his first day in the office."

"Yeah maybe, but I'm not so sure. We will just have to see."

****

The rest of the day went by with no more requests or run-ins with Mr. Thayer. No one saw him for the rest of the day. I'm not sure if he left early or was locked up in his office. He wouldn't need to come out for anything. He has his own personal bathroom. He also has Myrtle to get him whatever he needs like coffee or food.

I was glad to be home and out of the office for once. Ever since Halle and I took on the Sampson case I have been nose deep in contracts since. Halle, love her to death, but contracts aren't her thing, so being the good friend that I am, I took that on for her. Now that everything is set for signing on Monday, I have the weekend to actually relax.

I dug the note from B out of my purse. I stared at it contemplating whether to message him or not. After a few minutes I decided to message Halle instead.

> *Drinks?*
> *So down!*
> *Micky's in an hour?*
> *Yes. Okay if Andrew tags along?*
> *Of course.*

With plans made, I hopped in the shower. Just a quick wash to rinse away the stress of the day. Micky's isn't a fancy bar, so I decided on a pair of skinny jeans with an off the shoulder black silk blouse and I paired it with a pair of honeycomb Jimmy Choo high heels. I released my wavy strawberry blonde hair from its tight bun that I have been sporting all day. It is still wet from my shower this morning, so I added some mousse and scrunched up the ends. I added a small pair of earrings, a couple of silver bracelets and a silver watch. I refreshed my makeup with a little eyeliner and mascara to make my blue eyes pop. I then added a little blush and a little bit of pink lip gloss.

When I arrived at Micky's, Halle and Andrew were already there waiting for me. They were at my favorite table, the one in the dark back corner. I ordered a Cosmo before heading over to the table.

"Okay, now spill," Halle said with a glare.

"Spill what?" I asked innocently. I pretended to not know what she was talking about. After our meeting today with Mr. Thayer, I never got the chance to tell her about the details from last night.

"Spill now or wear my drink." She motioned her drink towards me as if she was going to throw it in my face.

"Ok fine," I told her and Andrew every last detail from last night. I told them about the big burly man, B saving me, him taking me home and me letting him have his way with me. By the time I was done, both of them stared at me in shock.

"Are you going to call him?" Halle asked.
"I don't think so."

"Why not?" both of them asked in unison.

"Because I don't even know his name. He doesn't know mine. It was a one-time thing."

"If he left you his number, he wants it to be a more-than-a-one-time thing," Andrew said.

"How is he even supposed to know who I am? What do I say when I text him? Hi, I'm the girl you saved and banged last night, let's meet up?"

"Yes." They both answered.

"I'm not going to do that. I have accepted the fact that I will never see him again."

"But you want to," Halle said.

"Of course, I do. The man made me feel things I have never felt before."

35

"I don't get it," Andrew said. "You finally find a man you are willing to enter your magic tunnel and he rocks that magic tunnel like it has never been rocked before and you refuse to call him. I don't understand women."

"Magic tunnel?" Halle and I ask at the same time before busting out laughing.

"It's either that or your honey hole. Beehive. Secret garden. Dirty dungeon. Snake cove."

"Oh my god. Stop," Halle begged as we laughed our asses off.

"Never have I ever heard a vagina called any of those names before," I said laughing hysterically.

"Then you definitely don't want to know the names I have for a penis."

We danced, laughed, and drank the rest of the night away. It was so much fun to spend time with friends and not be cooped up in my apartment or at the office working.

5

When I woke up this morning, I did what every human in the world does and checked my phone. To my surprise and embarrassment, I drunk messaged B last night and said exactly what I told Halle and Andrew I would never say to him. I was horrified. I was especially mortified when I noticed he had read it but didn't respond. With all kinds of thoughts running through my head of why he would read the message but not respond, I threw my phone on the bed and decided to deep clean my apartment. As I cleaned, I couldn't help but think about his reasoning. Maybe he didn't enjoy himself as much as I did the other night. Maybe he didn't like me. Maybe he regretted the whole thing. As frustration built inside of me, I needed to get out of this apartment. I decided to go to the gym and try and work some of it off.

In the middle of my workout, I got a text message. I hoped it had been from B, but it was from Halle.

Andrew and I are headed to Regents tonight. Want to come?

Regents is the club we were at last night. Thoughts of the burly man filled my head. I didn't want to go, but I also couldn't help but wonder if B would be there again tonight.

What time?
9
I'll be there.
Wear something sexy
I'll be the girl in sweatpants.
Better not be. I'll act like I don't know you.
Love you too.
Love you. See you tonight.

I decided to leave the gym early and I messaged my favorite hairdresser. If there was any possibility that I could run into B again tonight, I wanted to look my best. I decided on just a blowout. After I left the salon, I headed over to my favorite boutique to find a dress for tonight. After looking for about an hour and trying on dress after dress I finally found the perfect one. It is a white Bronx and Banco dress. It has blouson sleeves with padded shoulders and elastic cuffs. The sides are cut-out with a woven ring accent center. The fabric is lightweight crepe de chine with a tiered ruffle skirt with an exposed back zipper closure. Regents is a high-end night club, and this dress is perfect. The dress alone is over five hundred dollars, but it would be worth it if B got to see me in it. I also picked up a pair of twelve-hundred-dollar red Christian Louboutin's Astronomo heels. It is highlighted with a crystal-embellished bowtie adorned with a satin ankle tie. The pop of red is a perfect contrast to the white dress.

****

My Uber pulled up to the club at the same time Halle and Andrew did. Thankfully I wouldn't have to wander around the club looking for them.

"Holy shit," Halle said at the same time Andrew whistled at me. "Mama, you look hot."

"Thanks," I said as my cheeks started to blush. I do have to admit though, I do look pretty good.

"Andrew was able to get us into the VIP section."

"Nice." It was the only section in the club where you could get Champagne and tonight that is exactly what I feel like drinking.

When the doors to the club opened to let us in, the bass from the music instantly filled my body. Nerves also filled my body at the thought that I may see B here again tonight. As we made our way up to the VIP section, I kept an eye out for B. When I didn't see him, I felt a little disappointed, but I decided I wouldn't let that ruin my night. Once we had a few drinks in us, our favorite song, *Unholy* by Sam Smith started playing and we headed to the dance floor. The three of us were in the middle of grinding bodies. It didn't take long for Halle and Andrew to find someone to dance with. They were swaying and grinding their bodies with two very sexy men, but they didn't compare to B. I started thinking about him and moving my body to thoughts of him. I was dancing alone but I could feel him touching me. That is until a pair of hands wrapped around my body and pulled me into them.

He started dancing with me, and he whispered in my ear, "If you don't stop moving your body like that, I'm going to have to take you back to my bed and have my way with you again." The familiar sound of his voice caused me to lean back into him and grind my ass harder into his dick. He was already hard and ready for me. The feel of his hands on my sides in the open cut-outs of my dress instantly made me wet. My pussy longed to fill him inside of me again. I didn't stop grinding on him. I couldn't. His threat didn't scare me. I wanted him to take me home.

I looked at Andrew and Halle and Andrew had wide eyes. He then whispered something into Halle's ear and when she looked over at me her eyes went just as wide as Andrew's. I didn't have a chance to ask them what was wrong because B took my hand and pulled me off the dance floor. He took me down a dark narrow hallway. Once we were out of sight of everyone else, he pushed me up against the wall and crushed his lips into mine. I would never get enough of his taste. He grabbed me just under my ass cheeks and lifted me up, never breaking the kiss. I wrapped my legs around his waist.

"God, I could kiss you all day and that still wouldn't be enough," he said into my mouth.

"Then do it," I pleaded breathlessly.

He held me with one hand and the other found my breasts. With a hand full, he pinched and pulled at my nipple. I couldn't help the moan that escaped me. "Can I take you home?" he asked as if he needed me to say yes.

"Please do."

The black SUV was already outside waiting for us when the doors opened for us to leave. As soon as the doors to the SUV closed and the truck started moving B was kissing me again. Our hands roamed each other's bodies, trying to learn every part of each other. We seemed to have gotten to the penthouse a lot faster this time. Maybe it seemed that way because neither of us was paying attention to where we were going. The same doorman was there holding the door open for us that was there last night. Again, B handed him a hundred dollar bill and we quickly made our way to the elevator. As soon as the doors closed, we were at each other again. It was like a magnetic force that kept pulling us towards one another. We couldn't keep our hands, bodies, or mouths to ourselves.

As soon as the doors opened up to the penthouse, B picked me up again and again, I wrapped my legs around him. He carried me to his room without breaking the kiss or stopping to remove our shoes. Once inside the room he threw me on the bed and quickly climbed on top of me.

He slowly removed one of my shoes and tossed it to the side. He kissed the length of my leg before removing my other shoe and doing the same to it. He flipped me over and unzipped my dress painfully slowly. As the zipper moved downward so did his finger on my spine. The man was painfully building me up and I would need a release soon. Once the zipper was undone, he flipped me back over and roughly removed the dress. I wasn't wearing a bra again tonight since the dress had a very deep v in the front. I lay there in front of him exposed in nothing but the white lacy thong I was wearing.

"Your body is so beautiful," he said. I got up on my knees, so I was facing him. I lifted his shirt over his head. I took his ear lobe into my mouth and kissed and flicked it with my tongue. I then slowly trailed kisses down his neck and chest. I took a nipple into my mouth and flicked it with my tongue before doing the same to the other. I then threw him down onto the bed so it would be easier to have my way with him. I slowly kissed him down his stomach until I reached the waistband of his pants. I unbuttoned them and slid them down. I could see how hard he was through his boxers. His dick was begging to be set free.

I removed his boxers and watched happily as his dick stood erect. He was ready and waiting for whatever

I was willing to offer him. I moved my hand slowly up and down his shaft. His eyes rolled to the back of his head before they closed, and a moan slipped from him. I licked the precum off the tip before taking as much of him as I could into my mouth. I slowly sucked up and down while pumping him slowly with my hand at the same time. I could feel the head of his dick swell and I knew he was ready to come. I know he is expecting me to stop but I wanted to taste him. He wrapped my hair around his hand and started moving my head faster.

"I'm going to come if you don't stop," he said breathlessly. I didn't stop. I wasn't planning on stopping. He finally exploded in my mouth, and I drank every last drop of him. He was sweet and I could drink him every day if given the chance. He wasn't bitter like most men, and I knew that was due to his strict diet. "Oh my god," he moaned. He held my head on him for a few minutes longer before releasing me. He then flipped me on my back and got on top of me. "My turn," he said with a smirk.

He followed my lead and kissed me in the same way I kissed him. He started at my ear lobe and trailed down my whole body until he reached my center. He forcefully pushed my legs apart and gently kissed me between the legs. I loved how he was forceful but also gentle when it mattered. He quickly found my clit and licked me softly at first. He then inserted one finger then another. He licked and sucked me as he pumped his fingers in and out of me. I was quickly on the edge of my orgasm. The man had me moaning and practically levitating off the bed. With an explosion I was coming to his mouth. Just like me, he drank every drop that I had to offer him.

"Mm, you taste so sweet." He found my mouth once more and kissed me. I could taste myself on his lips and I was ready to go again. I wasn't done with this man yet. I threw him back onto the bed and climbed on top of him. I slowly inserted his dick inside of me until I opened up around him. I rolled my hips back and forth and bounced up and down until I was squirting my juices around him again. Once my orgasm was over, he threw me off him, flipped me over and pulled me up on my knees. He mounted behind me and forcefully thrusted into me. He wrapped one hand into my hair and pulled while the other gripped my hip. He fucked me as hard as he could, and it wasn't long before I was coming down from another orgasm. I have never been fucked like this. I have never been into the rough stuff, or at least I never knew I was. B slapped my ass causing me to cry out with pleasure, which in turn caused him to pull tighter on my hair and thrust into me even harder. We were both then pushed over the edge and both riding the high of our in-sync orgasms.

We were both out of breath and collapsed onto the bed. He snuggled up into my back and pulled me into him. Breathless and thoroughly fucked, we both quickly drifted off to sleep.

6

When I woke up B was not in bed again and again, I didn't get his name. There was also another note on the bedside table.

I had to run into the office for an emergency. I will be back later. There is a surprise for you in the kitchen. Please don't leave. I will be back as soon as possible. Please make yourself at home. I have left you some clothes in the bathroom.

-B

Again, the note was just signed with the letter B. I got up and went into the bathroom. There were a pair of black leggings and a gray sweater waiting for me. It looks like he went shopping. I hoped B wouldn't mind but I ran myself a bath in his oversized tub. He did say to make myself at home. I soaked in the bath until the water turned warm. I then washed up with his soap and shampoo, again hoping he wouldn't mind. Once I was washed and properly dressed, I went into the kitchen to find out what the surprise was.

There was another note on the counter along with a large amount of baking items.

Let's see if you can make me like sweets again.

Simple and to the point. I always loved a good challenge. It's one of the reasons I became a lawyer in the first place. After taking inventory of all of the ingredients I knew exactly what I wanted to make. I decided to take B on a world tour with my desserts. I turned on Spotify on my phone and started baking away.

I made Pasteis De Nata from Portugal. It is a traditional custard tart with a deliciously crispy and flaky pastry shell with a light dusting of cinnamon on top. I then made mini-Tiramisus from Italy. I had to make the sponge fingers before soaking them in coffee. The coffee flavored mascarpone cheese was so creamy and light, I almost didn't want to top it with the Cocoa. I then moved on to making Gulab Jamun from India. Imagine a deep-fried doughnut in bite size form, soaked in a homemade sweet syrup. Now imagine something that is even better than that and that's Gulab Jamun. I then made him some Churros from Spain with a chocolate sauce, S'mores from the US but with a twist. I made homemade Reese's and used those for the chocolate portion. I made him Lamingtons from

Australia. Lamingtons are traditionally made from a small square of vanilla sponge covered in chocolate and desiccated coconut, but to add a twist, I made a homemade raspberry jam and layered it in the middle of two small sponges of vanilla cake. I then made Malva Pudding from South Africa. It is a gooey sponge cake made with apricot jam and served with a creamy sauce or custard. I also made Baklava from the Middle East and Rum Cake from the Caribbean.

There had to be something within all of these desserts that B would fall in love with.

After eight hours of baking and another hour of cleaning, I was exhausted. But there was one more thing I wanted to do. I went into B's office and found a pen, a piece of paper, and a pair of scissors. I then arranged the desserts on the massive, oversized bar and made little notecards for each dessert with their name and where it was from. I then made a sign that read, *Come take a tour of the world with me.* Once I thought it was all perfect, I decided to take a break and lounge in the living room.

Thankfully, B was signed into his Netflix account, and I was able to quickly find a movie. I ordered a pizza and got comfortable. Halfway through the movie and half of the pizza eaten I fell asleep.

When I woke up the TV was off, and the entire place was dark except for the light over the stove. I was still alone. B hadn't come back. I went over to the bar to find my phone and when I checked it there were a few messages from B.

There has been an emergency with one of my clients. I must fly to Texas tonight.

Please stay there. I will be back late, but I would love to see you.

Order yourself some dinner on me.

Make yourself at home. I will see you when I get back.

Still exhausted, I contemplated going home or staying here. Once I checked the time I decided to stay here. It is well after midnight, and I am still so exhausted. I made my way into B's bedroom, stripped out of my clothes, and crawled into his bed. His bed felt like sleeping on a cloud. It was the most comfortable bed I have ever been in, but I guess that's what money could buy you. The silky sheets were cold on my body causing me to cuddle up into the heavy comforter. I felt like a caterpillar in a cocoon. And in a matter of minutes, I was right back to sleep.

****

The feeling of someone caressing and sucking on my breast drew me from the most peaceful sleep I have had in a long time. With the moan that escaped me I met B's eyes and in an instant, he was between my legs licking and sucking my clit. I moved my hips with the rhythm of his tongue. It only took a few minutes to send me spiraling over the edge and right into a climax. He drank every drop of me. He climbed on top of me and crashed into my mouth. He kissed me with such fever, need and want. He was as hungry for me as I was for him. We needed to feel each other. He needed to be inside me as much as I needed him to be there.

He inserted himself inside of me slowly, and said, "I wasn't sure you would be here when I got home."

"I almost wasn't."

"I'm so glad you didn't leave, baby."

Baby?

I couldn't help but play the thought over and over in my head as he made love to me. The way he moved in and out of me was different from the way he fucked me roughly the other times. He was kissing me, caressing me, making sure to take care of every inch of my body. This was more than just having a physical connection with someone. This was emotional. He was tender and attuned to my needs. The whole process was drawn out in the best way possible.

I was becoming sore and tired, but I couldn't get enough of him. Sleep plagued the back of my eyes, but I wouldn't let it come. I wouldn't give into the need. The ache I felt within my body was something I didn't know I was craving. I needed it. Wanted it. The weight of his body on top of me made me feel safe and protected. My skin was hot, and I started to sweat. Droplets of sweat started to bead up on B's forehead as well.

After at least an hour of him making sweet, sweet love to me I was ready to come again. I could feel him swelling inside of me as he was getting ready to come as well. He started to thrust inside of me faster and harder. The air around us became a small frenzy of energy and within seconds both of us came at the same time. He filled me with his seed leaving me breathless.

B crumbles like sand beside me before pulling me into him. He wraps me into his arms, and whispers into my ear, "I don't ever want you to leave my bed."

"How can I stay in your bed forever? We don't even know each other's names," I said, finally remembering to say something about not knowing who we are.

"What's your name baby?" he asked between kissing my neck.

"Bellamy. But everyone calls me Bells. And yours?" I asked, turning over to face him and kiss his neck. I was getting heated again and ready for round two. I climbed on top of him and slowly slid down his shaft. I rolled my hips back and forth slowly wanting to build the climax I was sure was just around the corner. It wasn't going to take either of us long to come again. I began to move faster back and forth and bounce up and down. My clit was swelling with the need to come again. I didn't wait for him this time. I came and felt my juices squirt around him. This caused him to release inside of me again. Both of us completely satisfied and exhausted, I lay back down beside him and lay my head on his chest. "What's your name?"

"Byson. Byson Thayer."

7

My stomach flipped and my heart sank. I knew at that moment that we would never get another moment like this. Whatever this is, it is over. Byson Thayer is the new CEO at Taylor, Johnson, and Thayer. He is my boss. And we crossed the line. What we have done is wrong on so many levels.

I jumped out of bed and fumbled around for my clothes. "What's wrong?" he asked, jumping up too.

"Do you know who I am?"

"No," he said, confused.

"My name is Bellamy Adams."

"Bellamy Adams?" he said to himself trying to place where he had heard that name before. "Oh."

"Yeah."

"Oh no."

"Yeah. Oh no."

"This was a mistake. You can't be here. You have to go."

"We have to talk about this," I said taken aback by his response. He had called me a mistake.

"No, we don't. We are two adults. We had sex. This can and will never happen again. You are just an employee to me. Now please take your things and go. I will have my driver take you home."

I was hurt. He said I was a mistake. I am nothing but an employee to him. He just made love to me and called me baby and in a matter of seconds I was trash. I was no one. I only knew him for a few days, but I was falling so quickly for him. He made me feel things in three days that no man has ever made me feel in my entire life.

Tears filled my eyes and I turned away to leave so he wouldn't see. I don't know how to just be an employee. I don't know how to work with him and not feel anything. I don't know if I can do it.

He had turned so cold so fast towards me and I'm not sure I could handle that.

Byson's driver was waiting for me when I exited the building. I didn't want to take the ride but getting an Uber at this hour was almost impossible. Plus, I didn't want to be standing here waiting for the Uber and having the doorman watch me cry. The sun was starting to come up by the time the driver pulled up to my apartment complex. I only had two hours before I had to be at the office and only four hours before the big Sampson Trading meeting.

I turned on the shower and got the water as hot as I could stand it. The bathroom was foggy, letting me know it was hot enough to get in. I stood in the hot water and let it wash away any pieces of Byson that were left behind. I washed away his sex, his smell, his taste. I had to be done with him. I had to move on. An impossible task, but one that needs to be done, nonetheless.

I blow dry my hair and stared at my puffy eyes in the mirror. They were bloodshot and swollen. I applied some mascara to try and hide it, but it just seemed to make them more noticeable. I didn't have it in me to care about what outfit I wore so I grabbed the first thing I saw hanging in my closet. Thankfully, it was a black pencil dress that formed to my body highlighting my curves. I slipped on a pair of red bottomed black heels. I paired the outfit with a black blazer, grabbed my purse and headed to what was surely going to be hell. I wasn't looking forward to running into Byson. I also didn't want to have that meeting he had scheduled for after the Sampson signing this morning.

I was a few minutes early so I decided to message Halle.

You on your way to work yet?
Right around the corner. What's up?
Meet me at the coffee cart. I need to vent.
Oh shit. You found out, didn't you?
Found out what exactly?
Nothing. I'll be right there.

Did she know who Byson was and didn't tell me? Had she let me make a fool out of myself?

"Hey," she said innocently as she gave me a hug. "You look like shit."

"I feel like shit," I snapped back. "What was I supposed to not find out?" I asked not giving her a chance to let me forget about what she said.

"The guy you were dancing with at Regents was Byson Thayer."

"Yeah, I know."

"You know?"

"Yeah, hence the way I look."

"Tell me everything."

"I don't even know where to start."

"From the beginning."

"I don't know. He was so different. He made me feel different."

"When did you find out?"

"This morning after he thoroughly fucked me, twice."

"Nice."

"No, not nice. He is the CEO, Halle. Do you not understand what this means?"

"Of course, I do. Listen, you fucked the boss. At the time you didn't know it was the boss. You aren't going to fuck him again, so don't sweat it. Move on. Find someone else to rock your socks off."

"You don't understand."

"What don't I understand? You don't have feelings for him, do you?"

"Yeah, Halle, I think I do. I don't understand and I can't explain it but there was just something about him. Our connection was instant. The hunger we felt for each was like none other. There is something between us that neither of us can deny. But how can we even do anything about it? There is no possible way for us to be together. We can never let anyone find out. We would both be fired."

"Damn, Bells, I didn't know it was that serious so quickly."

"I don't know how I let this happen. This is exactly why I don't date anymore. I should have known better than to let anyone that close to me."

"Bells, you can't live your life that way. Being closed off to possibilities is no way for anyone to live. You took a chance, you got hurt, now you have to pick yourself up and move on. We have to go get everything set up for the signing."

****

The meeting for the signing lasted longer than expected and our meeting with Byson is in ten minutes. I'm not ready to see him, but there is no way for me to cancel the meeting. I considered letting Halle go to the meeting alone but knowing her, she would probably give Byson an earful if she were left alone with him. And knowing him, he would probably fire her for it. He seems like the type of man to react first and ask questions later.

As soon as I walked into my office, my phone started ringing. "Mr. Thayer is ready for the two of you." Myrtle said without a hello. I looked at myself in the mirror before heading to his office. My eyes weren't as red or as puffy as they were this morning, but you can still tell I have been crying hard.

Halle met me at Byson's door, "Are you ready for this?"

"Not in the slightest. But what choice do I have?"

"I guess none. If you want, I'll take the lead."

"Thank you. I appreciate that." And I did. I was thankful she would do all the talking and I could be damn near invisible to Mr. Thayer.

"Go on in ladies." Myrtle said, wafting us in as if we were gnats that were irritating her.

Mr. Thayer was sitting at his desk this time but didn't look up when we entered the room. Halle and I sat in the large leather seats that were placed in front of his desk. The smell of old leather filled my nose and reminded me of Byson. I fight to hold back the tears that were trying their damnedest to escape. But I won't cry. Not here. Not in his office. Not in front of him.

"How did the signing go this morning?" he asked, finally looking up from whatever file he was working on.

"Everything went smoothly. Both parties agreed and signed the contracts without any problems," Halle said, answering for me.

"Ms. Adams, I thought you were the lead on this case?" he asked with a hint of resentment in his voice.

"I am."

"Then why is Ms. Davidson answering?"

"She is just as much a lead on this case as I am," I snapped back.

"No, she is your helper. This case was given to you. You are the lead. You need to answer any questions that are asked about this case."

"Sir," Halle tried to intervene in the conversation.

"Ms. Davidson, could you please excuse me and Ms. Adams for a moment?" Halle looked at me and when I nodded to give her the okay, she left the office. "I know we had a moment Ms. Adams, but that moment is over. We are professionals, and I expect you to act like it. I don't want this obvious mistake to cloud your judgement."

"Mistake?" I asked fuming.

"You don't honestly think those three days meant anything, do you?"

"No sir," I lied. "Why am I here? May I go?" I needed to get out of this office. I needed to be as far away from Byson as possible.

"You are here because no one can find out what happened between us, and I need to make sure you understand that."

"Understood, sir. May I please go?" I asked once more.

"One more thing before you leave."

"What?" I asked ready to run out of there.

"I have a case that I am working on, and I want you to be my partner on it."

"Why me?"

"One, you are the best in the office. And for two, I want you close by at all times so I can keep an eye on you. I need to make sure you don't run your mouth to anyone. Then and only then that I know you won't tell anyone will I let you out of my sight."

"I'm not going to tell anyone."

"Let's keep it that way. You are dismissed." I got up to leave and when I reached the door Byson stopped me and said, "Oh and Ms. Adams that includes your little friend Halle as well."

I didn't respond. I couldn't. Because if I did, I would lose my job. Halle was waiting for me when I left his office. "What happened?" I knew she could see the anger written all over my face.

"Nothing." I looked at Myrtle and said, "I am taking the rest of the day off. Will you let Mr. Thayer know, please?"

"You were just in his office. Why didn't you tell him yourself?" she asked with an attitude.

"Because it was a decision that I made just now. Will you please just let him know?"

"Okay, fine."

"Thank you."

"Okay, what happened?" Halle asked again once we were in my office and the door was closed. I told her everything Byson said and when I was done, she was just as angry as I was. "What a fucking asshole."

"That's being nice don't you think?"

"Well, what I really want to call him would probably get me fired. Are you really leaving for the day?"

"Yes," I said as I grabbed my purse.

"Want to have a movie night? I'll bring wine and cookies."

"Sure."

"Perfect. I'll see you around six?"

"Sounds good."

"What about dinner? I can order in for us," she offered.

"Okay. Chinese?" I really wanted pizza, but the thought of pizza reminded me of Byson.

"Yes ma'am. See you tonight." With that, Halle went back to work, and I eagerly made my way to my car. I couldn't get out of there fast enough.

8

When Halle arrived, she had a package in tow from none other than Mr. Thayer himself. She also had Andrew with her. Three bottles of wine, five containers of Chinese, a pint of Rocky Road ice cream, and a tube of cookie dough later, I was sitting alone in my apartment staring at the package Byson had sent me. When I got home from work, I put on the gray sweatpants and hoodie that he left out for me the first night I stayed at his house. I pulled the hoodie up to my nose and took a big sniff. I couldn't help myself. If I couldn't be with him physically, at least I can have a small part of him this way.

I opened the package and pulled the file onto my lap. There was a note that read:

I expect you to be fully caught up on the case by tomorrow. Meeting, my office, 7 a.m. Don't be late.
- B

I rolled my eyes and tossed the folder to the side. I grabbed my remote and angrily flipped through the channels. When nothing satisfied me, I clicked off the TV and tossed the remote. I grabbed the file and glanced inside. I wasn't too shocked to find that this is a multi-million-dollar case, and this is a high-profile client. One of the biggest distributors in the world is being sued for sexual harassment. I don't usually take on these types of cases, but what choice do I have?

I read over every inch of the file, and it looks like a pretty open and shut case, but we will be the losing team. Something tells me that Byson doesn't like to lose though. The employee has solid proof of the harassment. I guess Mr. Big Wig is trying to make it all go away.

I decided the case can wait for tomorrow. I was caught up enough to get by in the meeting tomorrow. I set the file on my nightstand and laid in bed. After tossing and turning for several hours, I finally drifted off to a restless sleep.

****

Meeting with Byson this morning had my emotions all over the place. I couldn't wait to see him but then again, I was also dreading seeing him. When I got to the office no one was there yet. No one usually shows up until right at eight. I knew it was only going to be the two of us and that made me nervous.

"Good morning Ms. Adams." Byson said as I entered his office. He seemed in a rather good mood. I can't say the same for me though.

"Good morning."

"Did you have a chance to look over the file I sent you?"

"Yes."

"Think you're up for the challenge?" There was a playful tone to him, and it was sending confusing messages to me.

"Yes, sir."

"Good," he said as he walked up to me. He pulled me into him and whispered in my ear. "I can't stop thinking about you, Bellamy."

"What?" I asked confused. I pulled away from him just enough to look up at him.

"I don't know what it is or why, but I can't shake you. You are all I think about."

"But yesterday you said…"

"I know what I said, and I didn't mean it. You were never a mistake. I want you. I need to feel you. I need to be inside of you."

"Stop," I said pulling away from him. "We can't do this. If anyone found out, that would end my career. You're a CEO so you will just get a high five. But me, I'll be known as the girl that slept her way to the top."

"It won't be that way. No one ever has to find out."

"So, what then, I'll just be your little secret to have whenever you feel like it. I'm sorry, but that doesn't work for me."

"Bellamy…"

"No, Byson. You are my boss, and it will stay that way. Yesterday you said we are professionals so we *both* need to act like it."

"Are you sure that is how you want it?"

No!

"Yes. That is the only way it can be."

"Okay. Then that is what we will be."

I wanted to take him up on his offer with every fiber of my being, but I couldn't, no, I wouldn't be anyone's secret. It was all or nothing for me. And right now, it's nothing. We could never be together. It just wouldn't work. No matter how badly it hurt to turn him down, I know deep down it was the right choice.

****

Eight weeks later

Everything with Byson has gone better than expected. I can't say that I don't miss the hell out of him, but professionally we have been getting along rather well. He has stuck to his promise and not attempted to pursue me again and for that I have been so thankful. I don't think I would be able to turn him down a second time. The case we are working on together is just about done and we can go back to normal. I have managed to talk our client into settling out of court and giving the plaintiff a very large sum of money for her trouble. They are coming in to settle in an hour.

"Hey babe, Andrew and I are going to Regents tonight, want to join?" Halle asked.

"I'd love to, but I have this stupid cold that won't go away."

"Come on Bells. You haven't been out in two months. It's time to get back on that horse and ride."

"I don't know. I haven't been feeling that well lately."

"Come on. It will do you some good to get out of the house a little bit."

"You aren't going to leave me alone until I say yes, are you?"

"Of course not," she said with a laugh. "What kind of friend would I be if I let you stay cooped up in your apartment for the rest of your life?"

"Fine, I'll go."

Regents was extra packed tonight. There were so many grinding bodies we could barely make it to the bar. Once our drinks were ordered, we found a small standing table in the corner. I wasn't feeling as sexy and confident as usual, so I wore a black asymmetrical neck, slit sleeve Bodycon dress to boost my confidence a little bit. I paired it with thick gold hoops and a gold bracelet on each wrist. I decided to wear my hair in a slick high ponytail and heavy smoky makeup. After everything that happened with Byson, my self-esteem was nowhere in sight.

Only after being in the club for a few minutes, two very cute guys came up to our table. One had shaggy blonde hair and blue eyes, while the other, the one talking to me, had dark well-groomed hair and dark chocolate eyes. He had a mysterious way about him that intrigued me.

"Hi," he said shyly.

"Hi."

"I'm Knox."

"Bellamy."

The DJ played a slow song, *The Joker and the Queen* by Ed Sheeran, causing Knox to lean into me and ask, "Would you like to dance?" He held out his hand for me and I gladly took it. Knox wasn't Byson, but he was still a very good-looking man. *Boyfriend* by Dove Cameron started to play and Halle and the blonde guy she was talking to joined us on the dance floor. I was grinding my ass into Knox starting to get into the beat when someone grabbed my arm and pulled me off the dance floor. Going down a familiar narrow hallway, I realized who had a hold of me.

"What in the fuck do you think you are doing?" Byson screamed at me.

"Dancing. What the hell does it look like I'm doing?" I snapped, not backing down.

"You can't dance with him like that."

"And why not?"

"Because I said so."

"You may be my boss at work, but you have no say over me here."

"You are mine and I will not have you dancing on him like that."

"I belong to no one. You can't tell me what I can and can't do. So, Fuck. Off." I walked away leaving him standing in the hall. The beat had picked up a little and I went back to find Knox ready to continue dancing. *Mamiii* by Becky G was playing. The beat was faster but still a beat used for grinding. Knox was a very good dancer and was able to keep up with my every move.

Halle grabbed my hands and intertwined our fingers and danced with me so she could ask, "Are you okay?"

"Yeah."

"What did he want?"

"He said I couldn't dance with Knox and that I was his."

"Are you fucking kidding?" Knox and the blonde were still dancing with us but letting us have our space to talk.

"No."

"It's been two months and he thinks he has a right to you? What a fucking ass."

For the rest of the night, we danced and talked with Knox and the blonde guy whose name is Carter. They were funny and made everything light. When the club closed at two, we decided to head over to Denny's for some pancakes.

"Whatever happened to Andrew?" I asked Halle as we sat at a table.

"He met some guy as soon as we got there and haven't seen him since.

"So, tell me something about yourself," Knox said.

"What would you like to know?" I asked playfully.

"What type of work do you do?"

"I'm a lawyer. You?"

"Architect."

"That's a very good job. Does it cause you to travel a lot?"

"Sometimes."

The conversation with Knox was simple. It flowed seamlessly. I could see us potentially becoming friends, but not something more than that.

9

It's been three days since I saw Byson at the club. Luckily for me, he has been out of town so there have been no run-ins at the office either. I am still so angry with him. What right does he have to claim me as his when he said we couldn't be together? What right does he have telling me who I can or can't be with? The frustration this man has built up in me is overwhelming. I want to punch someone or break something. I want to punch Byson.

Pacing back and forth in my office trying to walk off some of my agitation, I heard a ping from my phone letting me know I got a text message.

How would you like to have dinner with me tonight?

A smile spread across my face at the invitation from Knox.

I don't know. I have to check my schedule to see if I'm free. I text back being flirty.

How does 8 sound?

Sounds good.

I will pick you up. Just text me your address.

"What on that phone could possibly have you smiling like that?" Halle asked as she walked into my office.

"I just got asked to dinner?"

"By?"

"Knox," I said smiling again.

"How are things going with him?"

"We haven't seen each other since the night at the club but we have been texting the past three days."

"Wow. Really?"

"Yeah. Why? What about you and Carter?"

"What about me and Carter?" She seemed like she was trying to evade the question.

"Have the two of you seen each other? Talked to each other?"

"Maybe."

"Halle! Already? You guys just met."

"What? It's okay for you to do it too, you know?"

"When? Where? I want all the details."

She closed the door and the two of us got comfortable on the couch I was lucky enough to have in my office. "He actually came back to my place the night after we left Denny's, and he has been there every night since."

"Holy shit girl."

"I know. We just hit it off so well. He is funny and charming and so, so sweet."

"So?"

"So what?"

"How is the sex?"

"Honestly?"

"Of course. You know always one hundred percent honesty."

"We haven't slept together yet."

"Come again? You mean to tell me that this man has been at your house for three nights, sleeping in your bed next to you, and hasn't made a move?"

"Yes. I mean we have done some things just not *the* thing."

"Is he a good kisser at least?"

"So good," she said remembering the last kiss they shared.

I couldn't help but feel a little jealous. The last time I was kissed was by Byson and I still craved the taste and feel of his lips against mine. It has been two months, but I don't think any amount of time will ever make me forget the taste of him. Everything about him is imprinted in my memories.

"Will you see him tonight?"

"Yes," she said shyly as if I would judge her for it. "He is actually taking me to dinner as well tonight."

"Oh nice. We both have dates." A knock at the door caused both of us to jump followed by laughter. "Come in," I said, still giggling like a little schoolgirl.

"Mr. Thayer wants to see you in his office," Myrtle said.

"I thought he was out of town?"

"And I thought the two of you were professionals, yet here you are fooling around like children."

Halle and I both looked at each other before I said, "I'll be right there."

Great. The last thing I wanted today was to see Byson. Who am I kidding? I wanted to see him. I counted the moments until the next time I saw him. And this is why he frustrates me so much. The damn man is all I can think about, and I try to stay away from him and move on, but he just keeps pulling me back in.

As I make my way to Mr. Thayer's office, I practice in my head of how to handle being around him. I plan to be short and to the point. I *will* be professional. I will not let him get me emotional. I will not even make eye contact.

"Myrtle said you wanted to see me," I say as I enter his office.

"Close the door." There was something in his voice that made everything I rehearsed melt away. I closed the door as quickly as I could. Before I got completely turned around Byson had me pressed up against the door, his lips crashing into mine. All my resolve melted away with that kiss. The kiss was filled with hunger and wanting from the both of us. We kissed each other as if our lives depended on it. We both needed this. We both wanted this.

He turned me around, so I was facing the door now. He moved my hair out of the way and kissed my neck before whispering in my ear, "Tell me to stop and I will." My lips were sealed. I wasn't going to say a word. I wanted this to happen as much as he did. With my silence giving him the green light, he lifted my skirt until it was completely over my ass. He lifted his hand and spanked me. My black lacy thong was no help in cushioning the blow. It hurt but it also felt so good. "You have been a bad girl." He smacked my ass again causing a moan to escape me. "You have been disobedient." He smacked my ass again but this time on the opposite side. "You will pay for disobeying me." He spun me around to face him and grabbed a handful of my pussy. "Do you see how wet you get for me? This pussy belongs to me."

Hearing him claim me makes me feel things I didn't know were possible. It definitely made me want him even more than I ever imagined I could. Byson picked me up and carried me over to the brown leather couch that was on the furthest wall in his office away from the door. He put me down and said, "You will do what I say. Do you hear me?"

"Yes," I responded as excitement flooded my body.

"Take off your panties." I do as he demands. "Sit." Again, I do as I'm told. "Spread your legs and lay back." Without hesitation I do it. I kind of want to disobey just to see what he would do, but I'm also very intrigued as to where this is going. He rubbed my upper thighs and squeezed a little hard. He started trailing kisses up my thighs until he got to my center. He placed a kiss at the top and then licked all the way down my fold. "This pussy belongs to me." He licked his way back up until he found my clit. He flicked it a couple of times with his tongue and then again said, "This *pussy* belongs to me." He licked, sucked, and even nibbled my pussy until I was on the verge of coming. He had me right at the edge when he stopped and asked. "Who does this pussy belong to?"

"Don't stop," I said frustrated that he would get me right there and then stop.

"Do you want me to make you come baby?"

"Yes, please. Please make me come," I begged.

"If you want me to let you come, tell me who this pussy belongs to." To tease me even more he licked, sucked, and flicked my clit again with his tongue. "Who does this pussy belong to Bellamy?"

"You, Byson. It belongs to you."

"Good girl." He inserted a finger and when I was wide enough, he inserted another as my reward. He thrust his fingers in and out as he licked my clit. In a matter of seconds, I was falling over the edge and coming for him. When I was done riding the wave of my orgasm, he slid his fingers out and stuck them in his mouth. "Mm-" He moaned as he tasted my juices, "You taste so fucking good." Byson stood up and unzipped his pants. "Bend over." He demanded and I happily complied. With my skirt still up around my waist, he centered himself behind me and thrust into me hard. An uncontrollable moan escaped me with the force. He slammed into me so hard and so fast over and over again. I wouldn't be surprised if Myrtle could hear our skin slapping together. Byson was digging his fingers into my hips, and I was digging mine into the arm of the couch.

"Byson, I'm going to come."

"Then come for me baby. Come on my dick and claim it as yours." His words sent me right over the edge and I was coming again.

"It's my turn," he said as he started to move even faster and harder. It didn't matter that I had already come twice, because with the way he was pounding into me I was going to come again. "Tell me who this pussy belongs to."

"You."

"Who?"

"You, Byson. Oh God. Byson, this pussy belongs to you," I screamed as the two of us came together. It was the best orgasm I have ever had. When he pulled out of me, I fell forward and rested myself over the arm of the couch. I didn't care that my ass was in the air fully exposed, and I didn't care that my pussy was dripping with his and my juices. I was fully satisfied. He fed the hunger inside of me completely. He gave me exactly what I had been craving. What I had been needing.

I don't know how long I laid there but I didn't move until I caught my breath. When I finally sat up, Byson was laying back on the couch rubbing his dick while he stared at my ass.

"Like what you see?" I asked. I don't know where the abrasiveness came from.

"One day I'm going to fuck your ass." I think he could see the fear and shock that surely had to be written all over my face because he said, "Don't you worry baby. We will take our time. I will train your ass to take me."

"Train it?" I asked a little confused.

"Yes. I will start with adding my pinky and work my way up to my larger fingers. When you can take my middle finger, we will get toys."

"Um-"

"Are you trying to disobey me?" he asked with a dark gleam in his eyes.

"No. But-"

"There are no buts. I said I am going to fuck your ass and you will let me."

"I've never done that," I said shyly.

"Good." That was all he said before getting up and putting his pants back on. He walked over to his desk and picked up his cell phone to check it. When he set it back down, he looked at me and said, "Go clean yourself up in my private bathroom before you leave out of here." He sat at his desk and practically dismissed me. Anger and confusion filled me. I wanted to yell and scream at him, but I also didn't want to give him the satisfaction of seeing how this game he is playing affects me. I cleaned myself up and left his office without another word spoken between us.

10

Like an idiot I fell right under Byson's spell. I wanted to smack myself for being so stupid. I hated myself for letting him treat me like a piece of meat and I hated myself for liking it so much. Byson is all I think about, every day, all day. My imagination runs wild with the possibility of us being together again. I crave his touch constantly. I don't want to want him, but I can't help myself. The man is like a drug. I think the only way I will be able to move on from him is to actually move on.

I thought about canceling my date with Knox tonight since I just hooked up with Byson, but I decided it would be better to keep it. Knox is a funny guy. He seems genuine and sweet. He has the potential to replace Byson. Maybe. I don't think anyone could ever replace Byson. I'm not even sure any other man will ever be able to make me feel the way Byson does. But I am willing to try. If Byson is insistent on playing games with me then I need to try and get over him. Byson has the potential to shatter me in every way possible while Knox seems like he wouldn't have it in him to do harm to anyone.

I don't know what the date entails, so I decided on wearing a teal eyelet top with lace sleeves and a deep v neck with a pair of skinny jeans. I paired the outfit with a pair of tan heels. It was just dressy enough in case we went somewhere fancy, but not too dressy if we went somewhere casual.

While I was waiting around for Knox to show up, I got a text message.

It was a number I was all too familiar with. Fucking Byson.

I need to see you.
No.
No?
No.
What do you mean no?
Exactly what I said. No.
Why not?
I have a date.

There was no point in lying.

A date? After today?
Yes, Byson. I have a date.
No.
No?

I said no.
You can't tell me no.

I have no clue how to respond to him telling me I can't go on a date. Thankfully there is a knock at the door, and I don't have to respond. I shove my phone in the back pocket of my jeans and grab my purse. I am ready for my date with Knox to hopefully get my mind off the conversation I just had with Byson.

Shock and anger filled me when I opened my door.

"What are you doing here?" I asked, not hiding the frustration in my voice.

"Were you expecting it to be someone different?" Byson asked.

"You know I was. What are you doing here?"

"I told you I needed to see you."

"And I told you I have a date."

"Cancel it."

"No."

"No? Are you being defiant again baby girl?" I don't know why that question sent a wave of excitement straight to my pussy, but it did.

"I already told you I have a date. I am not canceling it."

"Yes, you are." His bossy attitude is so annoying.

"What makes you think you have the right to boss me around?"

"Because you're mine. Or did I not make myself clear this afternoon?"

"Yours? I don't belong to you Byson."

"Yes, you do. You are mine and you are crazy if you think I am going to let you go on a date."

"You don't have a say in who I do or don't date. You made yourself perfectly clear this afternoon when you dismissed me like I was some common whore. We can't be together."

"We may not be able to be together, but we can fuck. You love it when I fuck you. Why should we stop?"

"Because I'm not some toy you get to play with when you feel the need to do so. It's all or nothing and clearly there can never be an all. Now please leave before my date gets here."

"No."

"Byson, please." I sounded so defeated. I hated begging but nothing I said is getting through to him. "Please just stop this. I can't do this, whatever this is."

"This is whatever I say it is."

"You are the most frustrating man I have ever met." He walked up to me and ran a finger down my cheek. "Byson, don't."

"Don't what?"

"Don't do this."

"Are you sure you want me to go?"

"Yes, I want you to go." My voice was no more than a whisper. I was starting to lose all resolve. He was getting to me and if he didn't walk away, I was going to lose all control with him.

"Look at me, doll." I did, but I wish I hadn't. There was so much hunger in his eyes. There was a gravitational pull between the two of us and neither of us could control it. We needed each other. There just isn't any way this could work out. "Tell me again that you don't want me here." I couldn't say it. As bad as I wanted to say the words they wouldn't come out. Taking my silence as his answer, he slammed his lips against mine and all resolve went out the window.

We kissed each other as if it was the last kiss we would ever share. This kiss said more than either of us was willing to admit. I don't know how I am supposed to move on from Byson. How do I stop these feelings? How do we act like we mean nothing to each other?

It took all the strength I had to pull away, "I can't do this."

"Cancel your date and I'll leave."

"Don't do this."

"You want me to go? Fine, I'll go, but you have to cancel your date. I won't leave before that."

Honestly, I did want to cancel. I was so confused by everything happening that I needed time before going out with Knox. The last thing I want to do is hurt him. However, I really didn't want to let Byson tell me what to do. But I couldn't stop thinking about how Knox would feel if he showed up and found Byson here. So, I had no choice but to cancel and let Byson win this one. "Fine. I'll cancel."

"Good girl." After Byson got confirmation that I did in fact cancel he left leaving me with more feelings than I could handle. I didn't know how to process it all.

What do I do from here? I have no clue.

11

When I woke up, I had a couple of messages from Knox checking up on me. I had used the excuse of having food poisoning to get out of our date last night. I let him know I was feeling a little better but that I needed a couple of days to get back to one hundred percent. He was so understanding, and it made me feel like such a bitch lying to him.

I don't know what to do in this situation. I know I want to move on from Byson since there is no way we could ever be together, but I'm starting to think that is impossible. I like Knox. I do, but I don't feel the same instant connection to him that I feel to Byson. With Byson it's more than just attraction, or the connection for that matter. With Byson, it's cosmic. It's an unexplainable passion. It's heat and anger. It's soulmate level. It's love.

Fuck!

I am in love with Byson Thayer.

I can't love Byson. There is no way. I will not give up my career for a man. I won't do it. And I highly doubt he would give up his for me. He just became the CEO of Taylor, Johnson, and Thayer. There is no way he would give that up.

I have to try and move on. I have to fight against whatever Byson tries to throw at me. I can't let what happened yesterday happen again. I will wait a couple of days and I will ask Knox out. Maybe we can go to the club with Halle and Carter.

The thought of loving Byson scares me. I have never actually been in love with anyone. I have been in a long-term relationship, and I thought I was in love with him at the time, but now I know that was never love. Compared to how I feel about Byson, the way I felt about my ex doesn't even come close.

I do want to be with Byson though. I would do just about anything to be with him. Anything except giving up my career.

So, in love or not, I have to move on. I don't have a choice.

****

Feeling good with my decision about Byson, I decided to message Knox and offer to take him out tonight since I bailed on him the other night.

Was wondering if I could interest you in a fun night out to make up for bailing on you last minute?

What did you have in mind?

Regents with Halle and Carter?

Sure.

Meet there at 9?

Sounds good. Syt.

Sy.

Talking to Knox, I don't get the same overwhelming feelings for him that I get for Byson, but maybe those feelings will come with time. I hate this back and forth that keeps going on in my head. I need to accept the fact that I can't be with Byson and just move on once and for all. It's hard though.

I got to the club a little earlier than everyone else and I decided to wait outside for them. As I'm standing there waiting, a slick black SUV pulls up in front of me. When the window rolls down, my stomach falls to my feet.

"Get in," Byson demands.

"I can't. I'm meeting some friends."

"Still being disobedient, I see." He gets out of the SUV and walks behind me. He pulls me into him, my ass lands right over his crotch and he is already hard for me. Excitement floods my body. I know it shouldn't, but it does. "I said get in," he demands more forcefully.

"I can't-"

He cuts me off, "I don't care. Get. In," he says on a growl that has my feet moving towards the SUV.

I know I shouldn't get in the SUV with him, but my body and heart are at war with my head. "Where are we going?" I asked as he got in the SUV behind me.

"Just around the corner."

"Why?"

"We need to talk."

"I can't be gone long, Byson. As I said before, I am meeting friends."

"And would this friend be the same guy you were to meet the other night?"

"Yes, as a matter of fact it is," I snapped.

"Didn't I tell you; you are mine?"

"You did."

"And you decided to disobey me anyway?"

"I decided that since we can't be together, I will not be your plaything."

"Plaything?" he said, smirking at me. "You are not my plaything. You are mine. Every piece of you belongs to me." I won't lie. Hearing him claim me sent a wave of sensations straight to my pussy. I know I am falling right back into his trap, but I don't know how to get out of it.

"How can I be yours to do with what you want? How can I belong to you, but we can't be together?" I asked, almost sounding defeated.

"Do you enjoy our time together?"

"Yes."

"Then why is it so complicated for you?"

"Because I-" I stopped speaking. I almost told him that I am in love with him.

"Because of what baby girl?" He looked at me as if he already knew what I was going to say. "Say it. Tell me why it's complicated," he whispered in my ear as he scooted closer to me. There was no space between us, and I am starting to feel the need to touch him. I need to feel him between my legs. I crave him in more ways than one. "Tell me baby."

"Byson..." His name came out breathy which made a smile form on his lips.

He slipped his hand between my legs causing a moan to escape me. He grabbed a handful of my hair and pulled my head back exposing my neck to him. He kissed, licked, and nibbled on my neck while he rubbed my clit with his thumb. He spread my legs further apart to get better access. He slid my panties to the side and inserted a finger inside of me. "All of this wetness for me baby girl?"

"Yes." He inserted a second finger. He thrust his hand in and out of me forcefully causing me to ride the edge of my orgasm.

"Who does this pussy belong to?" he asks, sounding just as turned on as I am.

"You, Byson."

"Come for me baby girl. Let me feel how your pussy clenches around my fingers." With those words and his permission to come, I do just that. I am riding his fingers to help my release. By the time I'm done falling over the edge of my orgasm, I am breathless and spent. Byson pulls his fingers from inside me and sticks them in his mouth. His eyes roll to the back of his head as he sucks my juices off his fingers. I can't help the heat that rolls through my body. It was hot watching him do that. "You taste so sweet baby girl."

Not wanting to feed the hunger that was growing inside of me, I asked, "What did you want to talk about?"

"I think I said all I needed to say."

"Which was?" I asked frustrated.

"You're mine and you will do well to remember that." The SUV pulled back around to the front of the club and let me out. Before it rolled away Byson rolled down his window and said, "Make sure you go home alone baby girl."

12

When I got out of the SUV I wanted to scream. Not only was I now craving more of Byson and needing actual sex, but I am also mad at myself for slipping right back under his spell. I don't know what it is but when that man becomes dominant, I falter every time. There is something about being told what to do that just turns my insides to mush around him.

Along with being mad at myself, I feel guilty. I am meeting up with Knox any minute now and I just got finger fucked by Byson. I feel like I have cheated on Knox. We aren't together by any means. We are just two people getting to know each other, but it still feels like I cheated on him.

Halle and Carter pull up first with Knox following right behind them. As soon as Halle gets out of the car, she comes over to me and asks, "What's wrong?"

"Nothing," I say nonchalantly.

She looks at me skeptically and says, "Your face tells me otherwise."

"Fine. I'll tell you later."

Knox chooses that moment to walk up to me and pull me into a hug. I'm thankful he interrupted the conversation between Halle and me. I am not in the right headspace to work through it all with her right now. However, when his arms wrap around me, I feel the urge to pull away, afraid that Byson might be somewhere watching me.

We all head inside the club and I immediately head for the bar. I need a drink to clear these feelings and emotions swirling around inside of me. I ordered a shot of Vodka. When the bartender handed it to me, I shot it back without a flinch, and ordered another. I shot that one back and ordered one more along with a Jack and Coke.

"Whoa, Bells. You might want to slow down," Halle said, looking at me with concern on her face.

"I am," I said as I shot back my third vodka. I grabbed my Jack and Coke and handed it to Knox. I grabbed Halle by the hand and pulled her towards the crowd of grinding bodies. "Let's dance." I saw her look at Knox and shrug her shoulders as if they were having a silent conversation about me. They both looked concerned about me.

I needed to just be. I needed to dance and clear my mind. I needed to not feel torn. I just needed some peace.

I don't know why I thought I was going to find it on the dance floor though.

As I shook my hips and moved my body to the music, Knox came up behind me and started moving his body with mine. We fit together nicely but he doesn't feel the same as Byson.

Ugh...why can't I get this man out of my head?

Byson is in my every thought. He is in my every vein. He is in every fiber of my being. I can't get him out of me. He has consumed all of me. He has invaded me like cancer. I can't get rid of him.

As my mind wanders to thoughts of Byson the song changes to something a little sexier, *Have Mercy* by Chloe started playing and the beat of the music went straight to my body. I turned inside myself and just danced. Everyone around me disappeared. It was just me and my thoughts. Knox was still dancing with me, but I wasn't paying attention to him anymore. My mind has shifted to Byson and what I was imagining him doing to my body. By the end of the song my body movements were portraying what was playing in my mind.

Knox pulled me closer to him and shoved his dick into my back as he whispered in my ear, "Damn. You keep moving like that and I'll have to take you home."

Those words brought me back to reality. My eyes popped open, and I stopped dancing. "I need a drink," I said as I rushed off the dance floor. I headed over to the bar where I ordered water instead of alcohol. I didn't trust myself not to get wasted tonight and to not do something stupid.

We have already been here an hour and I'm already ready to go home. I can't leave though. I promised Knox a fun night out.

Halle ended up getting us a booth in the VIP section with bottle service. As we headed into the area, I noticed Byson sitting in a dark corner. There was a girl sitting with him laughing at whatever he just said to her. Jealousy reared its ugly little head in me. I sat in the booth so I could be sure to watch both of them. He hasn't noticed me yet. The blonde that's practically throwing herself at him runs a finger down his chest and I want to run over and break it.

Knox asked me a question but I'm not paying attention to what he is saying. I'm too transfixed on the blonde. She whispers something in his ear, and he shakes his head no. She pulls back making a pouty face. I want nothing more than to smack her in it. Her hand makes its way to his crotch at the same time his eyes lock with mine. He smiles at me as I stare daggers at the two of them. Byson pulls her hand away and shakes his head no to her again, and again she pouts. When she runs her hand over his thigh, I lose it. I'm out of my seat before I can even think about what I'm doing.

I'm in front of them in a matter of seconds. Byson looks at me with a shit eating grin on his face while the blonde looks at me and says, "Can we help you?" with an attitude.

"You can leave," I say to her. I'm not sure where this rage comes from, but I have to let it out. I have never been a violent person.

"Excuse me?" she asks, sitting up a little straighter. Byson doesn't say anything. He sits there and watches the both of us, curious as to how this will all play out.

"I said leave."

"I don't know who you think you are, but you need to walk away," she says, challenging me.

"Since you don't know who I am, let me introduce myself." I walked over to Byson and grabbed his hand. It's the same hand he had inside of me just a couple hours ago. I took his hand and rubbed his fingers in her face. "I'm the woman he had his hand inside of just hours ago." I'm sure there wasn't a smell left on his fingers, but I wanted her to know that she wasn't going to get her hands on Byson. He has claimed me as his and I am claiming him as mine.

She pushes his hand out of her face, "You are disgusting."

"I believe I told you to leave," I said locking eyes with Byson. "You have about two seconds to get out of here before I make you leave willingly or not."

"You can't-" I started walking towards her, making her stop speaking right in the middle of her sentence.

"One," I say getting closer to her. She looks at Byson as if he is going to stop me. "Two." I go to reach for her, but she cuts me off.

"Okay, fine. I'll go." She gets up, grabs her purse and looks at Byson and says, "Call me."

"Don't hold your breath," I say still locking eyes with Byson. The fury inside of me is begging to be released. I walk up to Byson and smack him across the face. "I'm yours?" I asked only inches away from his face. "I can't be with anyone else, but here you are with any fucking whore you can find."

"Baby girl, you need to watch yourself," he said standing up.

"Fuck you, Byson," I say as I turn around to walk away. He lets me go because people are starting to notice us. But this fight isn't over. We both know it. Soon, this will all come to a head.

13

I was so angry that I walked right past Knox, Halle and Carter, but I knew they got up and followed me out of the club. While we were standing there waiting, Knox asked, "Does someone want to explain what just happened?"

Halle and I looked at each other before Halle answered for me, "That was our boss. He and Bells haven't been getting along lately."

"That looked like more than them just not getting along," Carter said, causing a glare from me.

I turned to Knox and apologized, "I'm sorry. That shouldn't have happened. I promised you a fun night and I've ruined it." Knox just looked at me as if he was contemplating what to say to that. "I've had a bad few days and I just let my anger get the best of me," I added trying to smooth things over.

"The night doesn't have to end just yet," Carter added.

"What do you have in mind?" Halle asked.

"We could go back to my place. I have a nice little set up with a pool table and an in-home bar," Carter said.

As Halle says how fun she thinks that will be, I get a ping from my phone alerting me that I have a message. When I pull it out and read it, the anger inside of me just builds even more.

Tell them you don't feel like going.

I look at Carter and say, "Let's go." I don't feel like being told what to do tonight. Another ping on my phone...

Baby girl, you don't want to defy me.
Maybe I do.
Don't.
Or what?
I will make you pay for disobeying me.

I stick my phone in my purse not responding to him. The thought of him punishing me filled me with excitement. So, the only logical thing to do is to not do what he says. My phone pings again but I ignore it causing a wave of messages to flood in.

Don't. Get. In. That. Car.
Baby girl, listen to me.
You will pay for this.

I am going to punish you until you beg for mercy.
He better not touch you.

I turned my phone off after his last message. I am enjoying this cat and mouse game a little too much. I have finally decided on how to handle Knox and Byson. I'll continue to get to know Knox to see where it may lead, while having fun with Byson in the meantime. I can't fight whatever this is with Byson and for some ungodly reason, I want to see how far this dominating thing can go. I have never been dominated before but I'm learning that I really like it.

The most adventurous sex I have ever had was doggie style. I have never explored, and I've never had a guy try anything new. It was all missionary, me on top, and occasionally doggie style. I've been pretty vanilla when it comes to sex. I want to explore this thing with Byson. I just hope I can keep my feelings for him in check as I do.

14

By the time we got to Carter's house my nerves were so on edge for going against Byson. But there was also power in disobeying him. If he wanted me to do what he wanted me to do, then he would have to officially make me his. Until that moment I am a free woman, and I am free to do who or what I please. Now don't get me wrong. I have no intention of sleeping with Knox any time soon. Especially while I am clearly still actively sleeping with Byson, but I can still get to know him as a person. And I'm allowed to have friends. Right?

But why do I feel so guilty?

I want to turn my phone on so badly, but I know the moment I do Byson will win. Whatever power I hold right now I will lose. I will go to him. I will take my punishment like a good little girl, and I will bend to his will.

Carter's house is a lot nicer than I was expecting. It is a fair-sized modern home with a well-maintained yard. He led us through a small kitchen that looked like it had never been used and down into the basement. He was right, he did have a nice little set up down here. There was a pool table in the middle of the room just like he promised. To the left of the pool table was a brown leather couch that had recliners built into both ends that was set up in front of a large flat screen TV. I bet anything if I walked around to the front of the couch, I would find a game system of some sort. To the right of the pool table was the bar that Carter also had promised us. He walked behind the bar and slapped the bar top, "What can I get for the ladies?"

"What do you have?" Halle asked.

"Pretty much anything you can think of as far as beer goes. Wine? I have a select few reds."

"Liquor?" I asked, causing a smile to form across his lips.

"Now liquor. Take your pick and I can just about guarantee I have it."

Not in the mood for much and really just feeling like getting wasted, I said, "Vodka."

"Mixed drink?" Carter asked.

"Shots."

"Nice." Carter grabbed a couple limes from a fruit basket that I hadn't even noticed until he did so and cut them up into wedges. He slid the bowl of limes on the counter along with a saltshaker. He then lined up ten shot glasses. I'm well aware of the uneven number of people and shot glasses.

Carter starts filling the shot glasses with the clear liquid that I know will burn in a good way once I start pouring the shots back and Halle and Knox scoot closer to me. We each lick the heel of our thumbs and pour salt onto them. I add a little extra knowing I'll be shooting more than one shot. We each grabbed a shot and a lime. Carter says a few words that I guess are meant to be a toast but I'm not paying attention. Once the last word has left his tongue, I shoot back one shot, grab a second, shoot it back and grab a third and shoot it back before licking the salt off my hand and then sucking the lime.

"Holy shit, Bells."

"Again," I said, getting my hand ready for another round of salt.

"Are you sure?" Halle asked, her voice filled with concern.

"I said again."

"Yes ma'am," Carter said, lining up the shot glasses once more.

The only intention I have tonight is to get wasted and forget all my troubles. We did the same as before but this time I shot back four shots before licking the salt and sucking the lime. A warm sensation filled my body from the liquor. I sucked the juice from another lime before heading over to the pool table. Knox quickly followed me and set a game up for us to play teams.

"Guys against girls or couple vs couple?" Carter asked.

With the warm liquid flowing through my body and the filter loose on my lips, I quickly respond, "There are no couples here, so girls against guys." I didn't miss the flinch Halle made that she tried to hide behind the beer she was now drinking. I shrugged my shoulders and grabbed a pool stick ready to kick some ass. I was starting to feel a little loose from all of the alcohol I had consumed tonight. Things were starting to get a little spotty. So obviously another round was in order. "Another round Carter," I demanded.

"Maybe something not so strong," Halle suggested.

"I want Vodka," I slurred. I may be a little drunk, but I didn't miss the silent conversation Halle was having with Carter.

"Fine. One more round," Halle said.

Carter poured us all another shot but this time he only poured four shots. I don't know why this made me angry. Why was Halle trying to control how much I was drinking? She never cared before. "I need some fresh air. I am going outside," I said to no one in particular.

"I'll come with you," Knox said ready to follow me.

"No thanks, my guy. I want to be alone for a few minutes," I said as I patted him on the shoulder. I grabbed my purse and headed towards the same door we entered through. Once I was in the driveway, I grabbed my phone and turned it on, losing all self-control. I was itching to see if Byson had messaged me.

I was curious to know what he would say to me for defying him.

As soon as my phone was powered back on, it came to life with missed text messages and a couple missed calls from Byson with only one voicemail. I listened to the voicemail first.

Baby girl. Just the sound of hearing him call me baby girl had me squeezing my thighs together. *You will pay for your defiance. The things I plan on doing to you to make you pay for not being a good little girl will have you screaming my name and begging for mercy. You will cry and plead for me to stop. But I won't. I won't stop until you are completely mine. Do you hear me, baby girl? You will be mine.*

I couldn't help the way my pussy ached after hearing the voicemail he left behind. I'm not going to lie; I wanted whatever punishment he promised. I needed it. I craved it.

****

In my drunken stupor I tried getting an Uber. I was so ready to be done with this place and just get home. I wanted to go home, put on some comfy pj's, and curl up on the couch with some ice cream while I watch a movie and try not to daydream about all the things Byson could do for my punishment. The ache between my legs at the thought of him was instant and I was missing the feeling of having him there.

When I saw headlights coming down the road, I headed to the end of the driveway to wait for the Uber. When the SUV pulled up and the door opened in the back, I didn't hesitate to get in.

"How did you know where to find me?" I asked a little annoyed that he knew where to find me but also elated that he was here.

"I have more resources than the president, Bellamy."

"What do you want?" I asked, already knowing the answer.

"Didn't I tell you not to go with those men?"

"I didn't go with *those men*," I said, mocking him. "I went with Halle."

"I still told you not to go."

"And what? Now you're my daddy and I'm just supposed to do what you say?"

"Someone is feisty tonight?"

"Someone has struck a nerve."

"You will mind your manners baby girl, or I will have to punish you."

"Punish me?" I laughed. "Yeah. Okay, daddy. Punish me," I said seductively.

A growl escaped him, and I sat back in my seat. "Don't. Push. Me."

The rest of the way to his penthouse was quiet. I wanted to see just what punishment he would dish out, but I also didn't want to push him too far. Although, pushing him could be fun.

"Take me home," I say seeing just how far I can take this.

"No."

"Yes."

"No," he said a bit more sternly.

"You don't get to tell me when I can and can't go home Mr. Thayer. Or did you forget about the blonde that you were letting rub all over your dick tonight?"

"Someone sounds jealous," he said, smirking at me.

"No. You can't claim me as yours and expect me to only fuck you when you get to fuck whoever the hell you want to." The more I think about the blonde, the madder I am getting. The rage that is building up inside of me is something I have never felt before. I need to find a way to release it.

"Come on baby girl. Let me take you upstairs and make it up to you."

"Fuck you," I say through clenched teeth causing him to laugh.

"You know you want to."

"No, I don't." I'm lying. I want to so bad, but I can't give into him so easily. "I'd rather go home."

"Okay," Byson said as he got out of the car and slammed his door. He was at my side of the car in a matter of seconds. My door flew open, and he grabbed me out of the car and threw me over his shoulder.

"Put me down," I yelled.

He smacked my ass hard sending a sensation straight to my center. "That is for not listening." He smacked my ass again, "that one is for getting in the fucking car when I told you not to." Smack. "That's for ignoring me." He walks me inside and heads towards the elevators. Once inside and the doors are closed, smack. "That's for dancing with anyone other than me." Smack. "That's for talking back." Smack. Smack. Smack. "That's for smacking me in the club." By the time the elevator doors opened into his penthouse my panties were soaking wet and I was on the verge of an orgasm just from him spanking me. I was sure my ass would be sore tomorrow but tonight it was a pain I didn't even know I liked in the most pleasurable way. I wanted more. He walked me to his room still over his shoulder, but he didn't spank me anymore. Once we were in his room, he threw me on his bed, and I landed with a yelp.

"I hope you are ready for the rest of your punishment."

"Oh, that wasn't it?" I asked giggling.

"Your defiance drives me insane, Bellamy."

He flips me over onto my stomach and slowly removes each shoe. He begins kissing the bottom of my feet and so painfully slowly makes his way up the back of one leg until he reaches my ass and then slowly kisses his way down the other leg. It is erotic and torturous at the same time. He slowly removes my clothes and kisses every inch of my body making sure to stay away from the most sensitive areas like my nipples and my clit. By the time he was done kissing every inch of me I was in so much pain from the need to feel him inside of me. I tried touching him a few times, but he kept slamming my hands onto the bed above my head.

This is the most unkind form of torture imaginable. If this is my punishment, I don't want it.

"Byson. Please. I...I can't take it." His laugh infuriates me. "Byson. Please," I beg again.

"That's it, baby girl. Beg for it." He smacks my pussy hard, and I yelp with surprise and moan at the same time because the feeling was out of this world. The buildup he has caused in me makes me feel like once he finally lets me come, I will explode. He rubs his thumb in slow circles around my clit. My head falls back and the moans that escape me sound animalistic. I buck my hips trying to help him speed up, but he stops me instantly. "Now, now baby girl. A punishment like this can't be rushed," he said grinning.

"Byson. I need.... I have to.... I need to come. Please, Byson."

"Are you begging for my mercy?" he asked smugly.

Fucking asshole. I wanted to say no, but the torturous buildup inside of me needs me to say yes. "Yes, Byson. Please. Mercy." He dropped to his knees and pulled me to the edge of the bed. He swiped once over my clit, and I almost lost it right then and there. He swiped again, and again and again until he was fully emerged in my pussy, and I was thrashing and bucking on his face. "Byson. Oh God. Byson." Once I'm coming down from my high, he doesn't stop. He continues to lap up all my juices and has me riding another orgasm.

This time he adds two fingers to help me along causing me to clench around his fingers. Once I was satiated, he pulled his fingers out of me and put them in his mouth, sucking them clean.

"So. Fucking. Sweet," he said breathlessly. He stripped out of his clothes and climbed on top of me. He effortlessly slid me up onto the bed before placing my legs over his shoulders and slamming into me without warning. The hard feeling of him between my legs was something I had been missing so much. I clamped around him loving every inch of him inside of me. "If you keep doing that, I'm going to come faster than I want to baby girl." I clamped around him again causing a growl to escape him. "Fuck, Bellamy."

He pulled all the way out of me and slammed into me. He repeated this a few times causing a buildup inside of me again. He sank into me all the way until his balls were touching my ass. He stayed still for a second and leaned his head back just enjoying the feel of me. He threw my legs to the side of him, opening me wider so he could go deeper. Once he was as deep as he could go, he looked at me and said, "You better hold on."

Byson slammed into me so hard I thought I could feel his dick in my eyeballs. He moved fast and hard. The sounds of skin slapping skin, my moans and his animalistic grunts filled the room and was music to my ears. He sent me over the edge not once, not twice but three times before I came a fourth time with him. He collapsed on the bed beside me before pulling me onto his chest.

"Mine," he said, stroking my hair.

"Yours."

Exhaustion took us both into a beautiful ecstasy filled abyss within seconds.

15

When I woke up, I was still tangled in Byson. I couldn't help the smile that instantly spread across my face as I remembered last night. I also couldn't believe that he was still here. He didn't disappear in the early morning hours and there was no note to be found excusing him for his absence.

"Good morning," he said, placing a kiss on top of my head.

"Mm. Morning." I ran my hand down his chest and lower still until I found what I was looking for. Just as I expected, he was already hard and ready to go. I threw the sheet back and climbed on top of him. As I slid down his shaft, I noticed I was a little sore from last night, but I didn't let it stop me. Once my hips were rolling back and forth the soreness was well worked out of me. With the soreness gone, I began to pick up my pace. I moved faster back and forth and bounced up and down until Byson was on the verge of exploding inside of me. When

I knew he was about to come, I hopped off of him and headed for the bathroom.

"What the fuck?" he roared, causing me to giggle.

"That's for last night," I said over my shoulder as I disappeared into the bathroom.

"You're going to pay for that," he said, following me. Once he was in the shower with me, he pressed my chest up against the wall and pulled my ass into his still hard cock. "You think you can just give me this and walk away?" he asks in my ear causing me to giggle.

"What are you going to do about it?" I ask innocently.

He doesn't answer with words. Instead, he pulls my ass even closer to him and leans my upper body back against the wall again. He glides his dick along the entrance of my pussy before pushing in. "Now where were we?"

Byson took control of my body more than once before we ended up taking a nap to regain some of our energy. When we woke up the sun had gone down, and we had slept longer than we intended to.

"I love waking up next to you, Bellamy," Byson said, kissing my forehead and pulling me into him.

"I love waking up next to you too," I whisper back. Being in his bed, his arms, feeling his heat surround me makes me feel so safe. "I never want this day to end."

"Bellamy..."

"Yeah." I stared into his eyes waiting for what he wanted to say but no words came. Instead, he climbed on top of me. He kissed my lips softly and slowly. It was more romantic this time than the hungrier kisses he usually gives me. He starts kissing my neck and interlocks our fingers. He spreads my legs until he is lined up with my center and slowly enters me. He takes his time with my body. There is no rushing with his thrust.

"God, Bellamy. You feel so fucking good."

His slow movements are killing me. There is a frenzy building inside of me. My heart is reacting in a way that I have never felt before. He slowly grinds into me until what feels like hours have passed and then suddenly when we are both shattering around each other something inside me breaks. The walls I had built around my heart come crashing down and I'm left feeling vulnerable and exposed. A warm feeling soon replaced those feelings. It was inevitable. It was unstoppable. It was love.

There are no doubts about anything anymore. I am completely, undeniably, ten thousand percent in love with Byson Thayer. My boss. My lover. The man I can never have.

Byson lay beside me and pulled me into his chest. Tears threatened to betray me and fall but I held them back. "Let's stay here, like this, for the rest of the day," he whispered into the top of my head.

"I would love that Byson, but..." Just as I was about to say the words, my stomach growled loudly letting him know I was starving.

"Oh yeah, food. I've had other things on my mind. Haven't given much thought to that. Well, come on, let's get you some food. Besides, you'll need it to get your strength up for what I plan to do with that body of yours for the rest of the day."

****

Spending the day with Byson yesterday was magical. We made sweet, passionate love two more times before he fucked my body into oblivion. We are having an actual date tonight to discuss what all of this means and I'm so nervous. I don't know why I'm so scared. I'm hoping he will want to move forward with me, but we both have so much on the line.

I decided to message Halle to come into my office for lunch so I can fill her in on all things Byson. By the time I was done telling her everything she was staring at me with her mouth hanging open.

"Wow. I did not see that coming."

"What do I do?"

"You have to tell him."

"No way! I can't tell him I love him. We just finally made progress. And it's only a very small inkling of progress. If I were to tell him that he would run for the hills."

"You can't just let him string you along as a fuck buddy either Bells. That is how you end up with a broken heart."

"I know. I don't think I am just a fuck buddy to him anymore Hals. There was something different about him yesterday."

"Okay, so what then? Are the two of you a couple now?"

"No. Halle, listen. I know you are just looking out for me. I get it. I will be careful, I promise. I love him, but I am also very cautious of him right now. With a man like Byson, you have to take things slow. He doesn't seem like the kind of man that settles down easily."

"Okay. I trust you Bells. It's him I don't trust. I just don't want to see you get hurt." We sit in silence for a long period of time before Halle speaks again. "So, if he decides to make you his woman, how is that going to work? Would the two of you go public? Would he expect you to give up your career here for him?"

"I don't know," I said letting out a strangled huff. "I think that's what this dinner is all about. So, we can figure everything out. See how we want this to go. Hopefully get some insight into what each other is thinking about this whole thing." When I say each other, I actually mean him. I know what his body was telling me yesterday, what words couldn't, but I need to hear them out loud. I need to know exactly what he thinks and feels about all of this.

I don't know how I got myself into this mess. I just know, with Byson, I don't ever want to get out.

16

Byson is supposed to pick me up at eight for our date. Studying the clock, I notice that it is six, so I hurry off to the shower. I scrub every inch, shave every hair, and repeat the process one more time just in case I missed a spot. My nerves were going to get the best of me. This man has seen every inch of my naked body, and going on a date with him is what causes my hands to shake, my knees to wobble, and the butterflies to let loose in the pit of my stomach?

I fumbled through my closet until I found the perfect outfit. I decided on something simple but cute. I'm not sure where he is taking me so I wanted something that would be perfect for any place. The dress I chose is a knee length, belted a line, scoop neck, long sleeved dress. The skirt part of the dress is gray plaid, and the "shirt" part of the dress is black. They are broken up by a belt made of the same gray plaid that ties into a cute bow in the front. I paired it with a pair of black ankle boots. For makeup, I decided to do a gray smoky eye to flow with the outfit and I did my hair in long loose curls. Looking over myself in the mirror, I was starting to gain a little bit of my confidence back and the nerves were starting to disappear a little.

By the time I was completely ready to go, there was only ten minutes left before Byson would be here. When the knock finally came, it startled me, and the nerves were rearing their ugly little head again in full force. I straightened my dress, closed my eyes, took a deep breath and let it out slowly to calm myself before opening the door. When I opened my door, my smile fell from my face. Instead of Byson standing there, it was his driver holding flowers and an envelope.

"Hello, Miss Adams."

"Hi," I said, sounding more disappointed than I meant to.

"Mr. Thayer couldn't make it tonight. He wanted me to give you these," he said, pushing the flowers towards me. "He also said you should read this. It will explain his absence. Ms." This time he handed me the envelope.

"Okay, thank you," I said reaching out and taking both. He tipped his head to me and turned and walked away. I laid the flowers on the counter and pulled out the note.

Bellamy,

I am so sorry that I have to cancel on you tonight, but I have a family emergency. I have to fly back to Texas to deal

115

with a few things for my parents. I don't know how long I will be gone. I know we were supposed to have that conversation to figure everything out, and I still want to, but it will have to wait until I get back. I am sorry for having to make you wait. Please forgive me and don't hold it against me. When I get back, I promise to make it up to you by doing all of the dirty, nasty things I will be dreaming of doing to you while I'm away.

-B

Well, it looks like I won't be getting any answers tonight. Since I'm all dressed up, I message Halle to see if she wants to go to dinner. It's only a couple seconds before I get her response.

That mother fucker. When? Where? I'm going to kick his ass for bailing on you.

I couldn't help the laugh that escaped me as I texted her back.

Down tiger. He had good reason. Now. Paulino's. Be there in 15.

At least my outfit wouldn't go completely to waste.

****

When Halle arrived at Paulino's I wasn't expecting to see Carter, Knox, and Andrew with her. When I saw

Knox, my stomach fell to my feet. I hadn't planned on seeing him ever again since I bailed on them this past weekend. I guess I need to be the grown woman that I am and be honest with him and let him know that I am not interested.

"Okay, so tell me exactly why this bastard didn't show up for the most important dinner of your relationship." Okay, maybe I wasn't going to have to tell him anything. I glanced at him, and he didn't seem hurt, a little disappointed maybe, but otherwise he seemed fine. Halle must have already filled him in. I'll have to remember to thank her later.

I knew she wouldn't just take my word for it without thinking I was just making an excuse for him, so I reached into my purse and pulled out the letter Byson wrote me and handed it to her. "Here."

"Well fuck. Now I can't be mad at him."

"Nope," I said, popping the p.

"So, then what's the plan?"

"My plan is to just wait for him to come back."

"Girl, you really are in love, aren't you?"

"Completely."

"So, what's going on with you and Carter?" I asked her.

"Well, it seems we aren't as compatible as I thought we were if you know what I mean." she whispered.

"Oh."

"Yeah. We decided to just remain friends."

The waitress comes over and takes our order. When the orders are taken Halle, Carter and Andrew have broken off into a conversation. I decided to take this opportunity to talk to Knox.

"Hey," I said shyly.

"Hey."

"I wanted to apologize for the other night."

"It's okay. Halle explained everything to me. You could have just told me Bellamy. I would have understood. I'm okay with just being your friend...for now."

"For now?" I asked with a raised eyebrow.

"Yeah. For now, I will be the supportive friend. I will be here waiting for you if this doesn't work out between the two of you."

"And if it does?"

"Then I will say congratulations and be happy for you all while still being your friend."

"And being just my friend will be enough for you?"

"As long as I have you in my life, then yes. Listen, Bellemy. I know we have only just met but you can't deny that there is something between us. I know you are in love with someone else and I'm okay with just waiting for a while if that doesn't work out. I want to get to know you better. Be there for you. Just be your friend."

There is no denying that there is an attraction between us, but it is nothing like what Byson and I have. I don't have the heart right now to tell him that we will never be more than just friends so all I say is, "I'd like that."

With dinner eaten and the small talk over, I decided to end the night. I was ready for my warm bed. I missed Byson already and it hasn't even been twenty-four hours since he left. This is going to be the longest- however long he will be gone- time of my life.

17

It has been two weeks since Byson left, and I haven't heard a word from him. There hasn't been a single phone call. No text messages. I have texted him a couple of times, but I was just left on read so I know he got the messages. I don't know what's going on or what's changed but I'm starting to think Byson has changed his mind about us. Every time I think about how he is ignoring me, and I get mad at him for it, I feel guilty. He said he had an emergency to take care of for his parents. Maybe he doesn't have time to talk to me. I'm sure he will explain everything when he returns.

But then the more I think about it, the more I get mad. I know he has been checking his work emails and responding. He has been calling and talking to Myrtle. Why can't he respond to me? Is it only me that he isn't responding to? I hate feeling like an immature child that's seeking validation. This isn't who I am, but it's who he is making me turn into.

Ugh....

Men!!

Checking the ping on my phone, I got a message from Halle.

Where are you?
Almost to the office. Why?
Get here NOW!
What's wrong?
You will see when you get here.
Halle?
Just get here now!

My stomach immediately went into knots. I couldn't imagine what could possibly make her text me like that. I couldn't think of one thing that could be so much of an emergency to grant such a response. We are working on a case but it's a simple case. There isn't anything that could go drastically wrong with it that would cause her to rush me into the office like that. Racking my brain, the rest of the way to the office, and still I was unable to come up with any logical answer.

I stepped off the elevator and noticed a crowd gathered around Byson's office. I couldn't tell what the gathering was for yet. I spotted Halle and Andrew at the same moment that they spotted me. "What's going on?" I asked, still so confused.

"Oh Bells." Andrew said, looking at me with so much sorrow in his eyes.

"What is it?" I asked again.

"Um, I don't really know how to tell you this…" Halle got cut off by someone else. It was another woman; someone I didn't recognize.

"It was sudden. But when you know you know. Right darling?" the mystery woman said.

"Who is that?" I asked, looking at them both.

"When is the wedding?" Myrtle asked.

"Wedding? Who's wedding?" Halle and Andrew looked at me with so much sadness, not for them, but for me. "Who's wedding?" I asked again. I knew the answer, but I needed to hear someone say it.

Halle rubbed my arm up and down before saying, "Byson is getting married, Bells."

"No," I said tears filling my eyes.

"I'm so sorry."

"We had plans. We were going to talk about us," I said, shaking my head. "He can't be getting married."

"Obviously, everyone here at the office is invited. We would absolutely love to have all of you come celebrate our special day with us." Byson's fiancé said. Hearing her voice made me want to scream. I hadn't seen her yet and I didn't want to. I had to get out of here. I couldn't be here today.

"I have to go," I told them.

"Of course. I will cover for you today," Halle said.

Before Byson noticed I was there, I ran back to the elevators. Once the doors closed the tears spilled over and my heart broke into a million little pieces.

Once I was back in my apartment, I put on the comfiest pajamas that I owned and crawled into bed. I could not understand what happened or how this went so horribly wrong. I couldn't understand how I let this happen. I knew this was going to end badly but I let myself get attached anyway. Now I know why he wasn't answering my text.

I cried and cried until I fell asleep.

****

I woke to a banging on my door. I wasn't in the mood to see anyone, so I lay in the bed waiting for them to go away. There was a ping on my phone. It was Halle.

I know you are in there.
You have 5 minutes to open this door or I'm calling the cops for a wellness check.

I knew Halle would indeed call the cops, so I begrudgingly got up, wrapped myself in my comforter, and answered the door.

"About time," she said holding up ice cream and wine. When I didn't respond to her, she moved past me, went into the kitchen, and grabbed two wine glasses and two spoons. "Come on. Let's talk this shit out."

"There is nothing to talk about," I said walking over to the couch and plopping my sad, miserable ass onto it.

"The man you are in love with is getting married. I know you, Bells; this is killing you."

"Yeah, it is. But there is literally nothing I can do about it. He is getting married. One day my heart will heal, and I will move on. And like I said, there is nothing to talk about." I took the ice cream from her, grabbed the remote and turned on a horror movie. I'm usually a rom com kind of girl, but there is no way in hell I will ever watch another one of those movies. I'd rather watch people get slashed and see blood and guts go everywhere instead of seeing people fall in love.

Eh, love. What a pointless ass emotion. The only thing love is good for is heartache. Fuck love. Fuck relationships. Fuck men. And fuck Byson Thayer.

I hadn't even realized I had begun to cry again until Halle reached over and started rubbing my arm and said, "Oh Bells. I'm sorry Byson did this to you. He is such an ass."

"I really don't want to talk about him, Halle."

"Okay, we don't have to talk about him. Want to dance it out instead?"

"Not tonight. I'm not ready for that yet."

"What will make you feel better?"

"Honestly? Nothing. He shattered me, Halle. I just need time to mind the broken pieces." Having Byson show up at the office with his fiancé was like a slap in the face. He didn't even have the decency to tell me in person. A heads up would have been nice. I wish Halle would have just told me to stay home instead of rushing me to the office. She could have told me herself later. I hate that I found out the way I did.

It feels like my heart is being ripped out of my chest. Pain doesn't do this feeling I have inside of me justice. I don't know one single word that could possibly encompass any of the raw, intense emotions I'm feeling right now. He simply took a big part of me with him the second I heard his fiancé say they were getting married.

I remember that day we spent the entire day in the bed making love over and over again. That was the day my heart opened completely for him. That is the day I gave him my whole heart. Now…. Now I'm just supposed to keep going? I'm just supposed to keep going despite the fact that a piece of me is missing. I'm supposed to go into the office like nothing ever happened? Like we never happened?

He isn't there to hold me anymore. He isn't there to comfort me. He won't be there to make me feel something that I have never felt before. To make me feel things that no one before him could make me feel.

How do I do this?

I can't.

Not when I just went from having the whole world at my feet to now having nothing.

18

It has been three days since I found out about Byson's engagement, and I still haven't returned to work. I can't bring myself to face him. I am still having such a hard time moving past this. Functioning. Just making it through a single day almost feels impossible.

Sleep is scarce and scattered. When I do finally fall asleep, visions of what Byson's fiancé looks like haunt my dreams. My dreams are as tortured as my heart. Hunger is meaningless. My body is left without an appetite. I haven't showered in days, not giving two shits about my appearance right now. Right now, I'm not living. I'm merely surviving.

There is thunder constantly in my thoughts, hopelessness surging through my blood and a deadness shadowing my eyes. Confusion, anger and shame permeate my bones. My heart is singed and tremoring. The torment of my broken heart has left me empty and filled with dreaded apathy.

I toss and turn between victim and perpetrator. I search the ends of my heart seeking answers, exhausting all rationality. Memories of old times flash through my mind constantly causing the tears to flow like a river that has broken through a dam. No matter how much I search for the answers, I'm still left so confused.

Waging a war within myself, I know I have to go to work today. I can't put it off any longer. I will do everything in my power to avoid Byson. Hopefully, he will be in meetings all day and I won't have to see him at all.

I finally showered, but it was only to remove the smell I was starting to protrude and the grease from my hair. I threw on the first thing I found in my closet not really caring. I threw my hair in a bun and definitively skipped the makeup routine today. No amount of makeup would hide my blotchy, puffy eyes. So, makeup didn't matter at this point. I grabbed my purse and headed to the one place I didn't want to go.

My own personal hell on earth.

****

So far today I haven't had any run-ins with Byson. Just a few more hours to go and I will have successfully made it through the day without having to see him.

Just as the thought crossed my mind, Myrtle stuck her head in the door of my office and said, "Mr. Thayer requests a meeting with you."

"Tell Mr. Thayer that I am unavailable today." Myrtle looked at me like I had grown two heads. She wasn't used to people telling the boss no. Time for some changes around here. "Anything else?" I asked.

"Is that really what you want me to tell him?"

"Yes. I am unavailable for Mr. Thayer. As a matter of fact, tell Mr. Thayer that I will be unavailable for the rest of the week."

"Um-" She didn't really know what to say.

"That will be all, Myrtle. Thank you." I got up and shut my door letting her know this conversation was over.

I was finishing up an email when my office door flew open then slammed behind the one person I didn't want to see. Looking up over my computer I said, "I told Myrtle I was unavailable for you today."

"You don't get to be unavailable to me. If I call for a meeting with you, then I expect you to show up."

"And if I don't?"

"There will be consequences."

"Really, Byson? I think you stopped being able to punish me when you got engaged."

"So, you heard?" he said, sounding not only deflated, but sorry.

"Of course, I heard. What did you think would happen when you brought her to the office to show her off?"

"That's not what…"

"It doesn't matter. Why did you request a meeting with me? What do you need?" I asked, trying to change the subject.

"I wanted to talk to you about everything."

"Nothing work related then?"

"No. I wanted to talk about us and what all this means."

"If you don't mind, Mr. Thayer, I would like to keep our conversation strictly professional. Work related topics only please."

"Bellamy. Don't be like that. Please." He started to walk towards me, but I held up my hand to stop him. "Bells."

"Ms. Adams."

"What?"

"My name is Ms. Adams. You no longer have the right to call me Bells."

"Please don't do this."

Rage filled me and I could no longer hold back. "Don't do this? Don't do this?" I yelled. "You did this. This was all you. I was all in. I waited like an idiot for you. And you, you went off to Texas and what, found the first woman you could find and decided to marry her? Two weeks. It only took you two weeks to get engaged."

"Just let me explain."

"No. There is nothing you can say that can make this okay. There is nothing that will change how badly you have broken me." I couldn't stop the tears that started to fall. I wanted to at least look strong in front of him, but it didn't matter anymore. "I'm done, Byson. We are over. If you don't mind, I have work to get caught up on."

After staring at me for a few minutes, Byson finally walked out without saying another word and when the door closed behind him, I finally felt like I could breathe for the first time since he walked in.

A small knock sounded at the door, "Come in," I said, wiping away what was left of the tears that had fallen.

"Are you okay?" Halle asked, closing the door behind her.

"Honestly? It felt good to yell at him."

"I heard."

"How bad was it?" I asked, rubbing my hands down my face.

"It wasn't that bad. I could hear because our offices are right up against each other. I don't think anyone else could hear what was being said.

"This is going to be so hard. I don't know if I can work with him every day."

"You can do this, Bells. I will help you through this. You just have to stand firm. Don't back down if he tries to talk to you about it again. You were right to stick to being professional."

"I want answers though. I want to know what happened."

"Do you think those answers will help you heal?"

"I don't know. I don't know if it will help me heal, per say, but it might help me understand."

"Is understanding worth knowing the truth?"

"Maybe. I don't know."

"If you have to know the answers so badly maybe meet him for coffee or something. Somewhere public."

"Yeah, maybe. I want the answers but I'm not sure if I'm ready for a one-on-one with him right now."

Halle left me to finish up my work for the day, but I didn't get any work done. All I could think about was Byson and by the time the day was over I was left more confused than when the day had started.

19

I was spending another night at home wrapped in my comforter in my comfy pjs, watching horror movies when a knock sounded at the door. I was expecting it to be Halle coming over to check on me after today, but when I opened the door, I was shocked at who stood on the other side.

"What are you doing here, Byson?"

"Can I come in?"

"No."

"Please, Bellamy. We need to talk about this."

Reluctantly, I moved out of the way and let him in. I walked over to the couch and flopped back down on it not offering him to join me. He stood in the middle of the living room contemplating where to sit before he took a seat at the other end of the couch opposite me.

"Horror movies? I didn't take you as a horror movie kind of girl."

"Well, I wasn't until recently."

"Oh," he said, knowing the change was because of him.

"So…"

"So?"

"You said we needed to talk. So, talk."

"I never meant to hurt you. I want you to know that first of all. I am really sorry for all of this." When he realized I wasn't going to respond, he continued talking. "My parents had an emergency and I had to go help them. I didn't realize that the emergency would cost me you."

"What are you talking about? Why would your parents have anything to do with me?" I asked, becoming even more confused.

"They don't per say. But what they asked of me, would cause me to lose you forever."

"What kind of emergency did your parents have?"

"What I am about to tell you, you cannot repeat Bellamy."

"Okay."

"I mean it."

"I said okay," I snapped, getting annoyed at him.

"My dad isn't a good man. I won't go into detail, but my dad owes a very bad person a lot of money. He didn't have the money to pay this man back. He threatened to kill my mother if he didn't pay. That's when my mom called me. I flew down to pay the man myself but when he found out who I was, he didn't want my money. He wanted something else. Or well, his daughter wanted something else instead."

"You?"

"Yes. She wanted me. She begged her father to take me instead of the money. He agreed. He said I had to marry his daughter, or he would kill both of my parents. I didn't have a choice, Bellamy. I didn't want this. I didn't want her. I wanted you. I still want you." I didn't know what to say. I couldn't respond. I knew there were bad people in the world but stuff like this only happens in books or movies. This doesn't happen to real people. Does it? "You have to trust me when I say I didn't want any of this."

"But…how…Is there no way to get out of it?"

"None that I could find."

"Who are these people, Byson?"

"I can't tell you that. It's for your own protection." He scooted closer to me on the couch and ran a finger down the side of my face. "I had every intention of coming back here and telling you that I wanted to be with you. I wanted to make this work. I have enjoyed every second of our time together and I will always cherish every moment I have had with you. I fell in love with you Bellamy. And I wish so damn much that things could be different." A sob broke from me at his words. I couldn't believe what he was saying to me. But it didn't matter. "Shhh…don't cry baby. I'm so sorry. I'm so damn sorry I hurt you. I hate that I did this to you."

"Me too," I whispered. I don't know why I was going to do this to myself, but I needed his touch just as much as I needed air to breathe. "How long before you have to go?" I asked fisting his hair.

He looked at me with knowing in his eyes and said, "Are you sure you want to do this?"

"I need you, Byson. Even if it is one last time. I need you."

"I need you too, baby. More than you know."

He slammed his lips into me causing a moan to slip out between our kisses. It was the most passionate kiss shared between us yet. But that's because this is the last kiss. The goodbye kiss. The kiss to end it all. I pulled away from him, stood up, grabbed his hand and led us to the bedroom.

"Bellamy, I have to ask you one more time…Are you sure you want to do this?"

"No," I said honestly. "Doing this will kill me tomorrow, but I need this, Byson. I need you."

Without another word, he lifted my shirt over my head exposing my bare chest to him. He started kissing my neck softly and slowly trailed his way down my collar bone and my chest until he reached the peak of my breast. He sucked in my rosy, pink nipple into his mouth causing me to suck in a breath of ecstasy. He grabbed my other breast and kneaded it in his hand. The way he was touching me and sucking on my nipple was causing a fire to burn inside of me.

"Lay down for me baby girl," he said as he laid me back on the bed. He slid my pants down my legs and started kissing them from my feet up until he got to my panties where he used his teeth to remove them. He kissed the hood of my vagina and said, "Mm...I have missed you so much baby girl." He spread my legs apart and smothered me with kisses before running his tongue through my slit. "Mm...you taste so good." He licked at my clit until I was levitating with pleasure. He lapped up my juices not missing a single drop. "I have to have you, Bellamy. Can I have you?"

"Yes. Yes, Byson. Please," I begged, needing to feel him inside of me.

With one fell swoop Byson scooted me up onto the bed and climbed on top of me. He was so fast I didn't even see him remove his clothes. Or I was just so high on my release I wasn't paying attention. He slid the tip of his dick along my pussy before slamming into me. He thrust into me hard and fast. We were both filled with so much need and hunger for one another. There was a rush, a passion that needed to be filled between the two of us and we couldn't waste another second. We needed to be in this moment together even if this is the last moment we would ever spend together.

"I'm coming, Byson," I moaned as he slammed into me faster and harder. When I was coming down off my high, he flipped me over and slammed into me from behind. He grabbed hold of my hips to hold me into place to keep me from flying forward at his hard thrust.

I was practically screaming with ecstasy with each hard hit he gave me. It wasn't long before both of us were riding a wave of pleasure and our bodies jerked with a release that sent both of us crashing to the bed breathless and exhausted.

The pain of this will kill me tomorrow, but tonight I will live in the moment of shattered promises.

20

It has been a week since Byson was last here. The smell of him still lingers on my pillow reminding me of the last time we spent together. It is a memory I will cherish forever. It was hard letting him go, but neither of us had a choice. He is bound to his fiancé, or his parents will be killed by some bad man, even as ridiculous as that sounds. And I just have to accept that and move on. There is nothing I can do about it.

My phone pinged letting me know I had a text message. It was from Halle.

Hey Bells, I'm grabbing coffee before work. Want anything?

No thanks. Not feeling that great today. Think I'll just stick to water.

Food?

No. Have some crackers in my bag. Feels like I won't be able to hold much down.

Okay. Sys!
Sy.

The past couple mornings I have been waking up nauseous. I think it has a lot to do with the amount of stress I'm under with this whole thing with Byson. We have, for the most part, stayed away from each other. We aren't exactly avoiding each other; we just know it hurts too damn bad not being able to be together so we choose to not see one another if we can help it.

When I step off the elevator into the office, I hear her voice before I see her. I still don't know what she looks like, but I would know that voice anywhere. Byson's fiancé is back in the office, and I couldn't for the life of me understand why she would be here. Regardless of knowing what she sounded like, I wasn't ready to know what she looked like. My imagination was already running wild with possibilities of how perfect she looks, and my heart isn't ready for that reality yet.

I made my way to my office with my head down. I didn't want to take any chances in seeing her. I wasn't in my office ten minutes before Halle came in, closing my door behind her.

"Oh my God, what is she even doing here?"

"Don't know. Don't care."

"How are you this calm right now?"

"What am I supposed to do, Halle? Cry? I'm all cried out, thanks. Fight her? I think I'm a little too grown for that. There is nothing I can do about any of this. Accept it."

"So, that's it? You're just going to accept him marrying her?"

"What else can I do?"

"Did you ever find out why he is marrying her in the first place?" I didn't answer her, and I couldn't look her in the eye. I hadn't told her what Byson told me that night when he came over to explain everything and I hadn't yet thought of a good enough lie to cover for him. "You bitch. Tell me everything."

"I can't, Halle. I promised I wouldn't tell anyone."

"No. You don't get to do that. You don't get to hold his secrets for him while he gets to break your heart. Now spill."

"Halle." I looked at her pleadingly.

"No, Bells. Spill. Now."

"If I tell you, you have to promise that you won't tell anyone."

"Scouts honor."

"You were never a scout."

"Fine. I swear I won't tell a soul."

"Not even Andrew?"

"Not even Andrew." I filled her in on everything Byson told me and by the time I was done she stared at me in shock. "Wow."

"Yeah. I know. And now you see that there is nothing I can do."

"Bullshit," she said, jumping to her feet.

"What do you mean, bullshit?"

"We need to find out who she is and then we find out who her father is."

"And then what?"

"Then we take those mother fuckers out."

I couldn't help the laugh that escaped me. "Take them out? Like hire a hitman?"

"No. We are lawyers, Bells. And what are lawyers good at?"

"I don't know. What?"

"Digging shit up on bad people. It's time we put our skills to the test, and we get your man back."

"Okay. How do we do this?" I ask, getting excited at the possibility of fixing this situation for Byson and in the hopes that I could eventually get him back.

We spent the better part of the morning trying to come up with a good plan to fix everything, but we didn't get very far without having a name to go on.

****

After my lunch of crackers and Sprite, Myrtle stuck her head in my office and said, "Ms. Gabrielle Delacroix would like to schedule a meeting with you Ms. Adams."

"Who?" I asked, confused. "Is she a new client?"

"No. She is the fiancé of Mr. Thayer."

"Oh. Um. Do you happen to know why she would like a meeting, Myrtle?"

"No ma'am. I was just asked to schedule a meeting between the two of you."

"Give me a few minutes and I'll have Andrew set it up with you."

She nodded her head in agreement before backing out of my doorway. I immediately picked up my phone and texted Halle.

Fiancé's name is Gabrielle Delacroix.
She wants a meeting with me.
What do I do?

It was a couple minutes before Halle responded and I thought my heart was going to beat out of my chest.

I'll see what I can find on her right away. Have the meeting.

I call Andrew and ask him to speak to Myrtle about setting up the meeting. He called me back a few minutes later and said that the meeting would be taking place this afternoon. I wanted to scream at him. I was expecting him to schedule the meeting for next week, not in the next hour.

Fuck!

If only I could run away and avoid the whole thing all together. But I guess knowing your enemy is better than not knowing them at all.

21

I watched the clock on my wall tick by in anticipation waiting until Gabrielle arrived. I don't know why I am so nervous to see her or why my heart feels like it is about to beat out of my chest, but the closer the time gets to her arrival, the more my knees bounce, and my hands shake.

Halle pokes her head around the corner, "Want me to sit in?"

"No. I will be fine."

"Are you sure? You look like you are about to throw up all over the place Bells."

"I'll be fine. I'm just so nervous. Do you think she knows about Byson and me?"

"How could she? No one here knew about the two of you."

"Then what could she possibly want?"

"I don't know, but I'm just next door if you need me."

"Thanks, Halle."

"Any time, Bells."

Gabrielle knocked on my door before walking in and closing it behind her. She was strikingly beautiful. She had long dark hair that flowed down her back. Her skin looked sun kissed and almost had an unnatural glow to it. She didn't wear a lot of makeup but just enough to accentuate her natural beauty. She is absolutely stunning. I don't understand why Byson would be upset to be with her. She looks like every man's wet dream.

"Ms. Adams-"

"Bellamy. You can call me Bellamy," I said cutting her off.

"I am Byson's fiancé, Gabrielle. I have heard so much about you and the work you do here. I just had to come meet you myself."

"It's nice to meet you," I lied. "What can I do for you today, Ms. Delacroix?" I asked, wanting to get this meeting over with.

Gabrielle's face turned to stone before speaking to me again. "I want you to stay away from my fiancé."

"Excuse me?" I asked, more than a little confused.

"I know who you are, Bellamy. Did you think I just accidentally chose to tie myself to Byson? No. I have been studying him for a long time now, waiting for the perfect moment to fall into his arms. I had the perfect plan until you came along. A chance encounter was supposed to get me into his bed, then I would win my

144

way to his heart. But you. You had to come along and mess everything up."

"Wait. What?"

"From that first dance with you, Byson was hooked on you. I personally don't see why, but I thought, let him fuck you and get you out of his system. But then he just kept fucking you. I saw how the two of you were getting close. I had to do something. I had to get him away from you before he fell in love with you. But as fate would have it, daddy dearest led him right to me."

"How do you know about us?" I asked, still not able to connect the dots.

"Let me start from the beginning for you so you can fully understand." Gabrielle took a seat in one of the chairs in front of my desk. "I have known Byson since college. He wouldn't know me though. I was not the same woman then that I am now. He never noticed me, but I surely noticed him. I was so in love with him. He was all I thought about from the moment I woke up to the moment I went to sleep. I was a shy girl then and I didn't have the nerve to speak to him let alone ask him out. Even if I did, he wouldn't give a girl like me the time of day.

When I heard Byson became the new CEO of this law firm all of those feelings came crashing back. Like I said I am a different woman now than I was then. I am not the shy, timid little girl I used to be. I deserve a man like Byson, and I will not let a woman like you take him from me again."

"None of that explains how you know about Byson and me."

"When I heard about Byson getting this job and moving here, I hired a private investigator to follow him around. I needed to know what his likes were, where he liked to eat most, where he hung out, if he went to clubs or bars. I needed them to find me any information that I could use to create a chance meeting with him. I was at the club the first time the two of you met. That was the night I planned for my first accidental run in with him. But there you were. You screwed everything up.

I thought he was just going to take you home, fuck you and send you on your way. But no. You kept showing up. Because you were always around there was never a time that I could run into him.

Thankfully his perfect little family isn't so perfect though. Good old daddy thought he could screw over my father. Little did he know my father isn't one to be fucked over."

"Who exactly is your father?" I asked fishing for information.

"Adrian Delacroix."

"And who is he? Why would he be someone no one would want to fuck with?"

"Because he is one of the biggest organized crime bosses in France. He is the head of Le Milieu. When I found out Byson's father was in debt to my father, I knew this was my second chance to get to Byson. I convinced my father to make Byson marry me instead.

He didn't want to at first, but my father can be very persuasive. All it took was a threat to kill dear old mommy and he was all mine."

"You're a bitch. Byson will never love you. Not the way he loves me."

Gabrielle got up, walked around my desk, and sat on top of it right in front of me. She placed her legs on either side of me caging me in. "See, that is where you are wrong. It will take time, but Byson will love me. Especially when I start giving him children. He will soon forget all about you, Bellamy. I mean I don't see what the appeal with you is anyway. You are very plain. Very simple. Unless…" She scooted to the edge of the desk and rolled me in closer to her. "Let me see if this is what the fuss is all about." She unbuttoned my pants and dove her hand inside so fast I didn't have time to object. She slid her fingers inside of me and moved them around causing a moan to escape me, my body betraying me. She slowly removed her fingers from inside my pants and put them to her mouth. She sucked her fingers clean and looked at me with a twinkle in her eye, "Yes. That's it then. You are rather delicious, Ms. Adams. Mm…maybe you can come play with me and Byson sometime."

"I would never be with you like that," I spat, causing her to laugh.

"Okay, fine. Let's get to the real reason I'm here then." She stood up and towered over me in my chair. She got so close to my face I could feel her breath on my lips. "I want you to quit. I don't want you to work here anymore. I want you as far away from Byson as possible." She stood up and walked around to the other side of my desk. "Do we understand each other?"

"No. I'm not going to quit my job just because you are insecure in an engagement that you forced on someone."

"I'm not sure you heard me. If you don't quit quietly, I will expose both of you to the board and neither of you will have a job. I have all the proof I need to expose you and to never have you work in this city again. Do I make myself clear now?"

Defeated, I said, "Crystal."

She clapped her hands together and said, "Perfect. I expect you to have your things cleared out by the end of the day. Byson doesn't need the distraction of having you here when we have a wedding to plan."

"You won't even allow me to put in a notice?" I asked dumbfounded.

"There is no need for formalities. Be out by the end of the day." She walked out of my office as if she just became President of the United States.

22

After Gabrielle left my office, I sat at my desk with my head in my hands for a few minutes going over everything that just happened. Giving up my job for Byson was one thing I was never willing to do, but when it came to having to choose between ruining his life and my career, I would give it up in a heartbeat. Gabrielle is a raging bitch, and I can't stand the thought of him having to marry someone like her. I could find a job anywhere, but Byson could never get his reputation back once it was ruined.

I started grabbing the few things I have in the office. It isn't much just a laptop, a notebook, and my coffee mug. I didn't need a box to carry my things out so no one would know I was leaving for good instead of just for the day. I grabbed all of the files from my desk drawer that I am currently working on and wrote a note. I grabbed my bag, the files and the note and headed out of my office. I headed over to Andrew's desk and said,

149

"Once I am in the elevator, wait ten minutes and take these files and this note to Halle."

"That's not cryptic at all," he says.

"Please, Andrew. Just do this for me."

"Okay, but I expect an explanation later."

"Once Halle gets the note, she will be able to explain." I started to walk away but turned around and said, "I really enjoy working with you Andrew." He smiled and I left. Once I was in the confines of the elevator tears started to prick at the edges of my eyes. I wouldn't allow them to fall here. No. Gabrielle wouldn't get that satisfaction. These tears would be saved for the privacy of my home.

Ten minutes later my phone is blowing up. I don't have the heart to answer it right now, so I turn it off. The cab ride home is quick considering I don't remember any of it. I'm too lost inside of my thoughts to notice anything passing by. Once home, I lock myself inside and let the weight of today take over.

The tears come faster than I'm prepared for. A sob breaks from my chest causing me to double over. I crumple to the floor in a heap. The pain is too much to bear.

I sit there on the floor in a shattered, crying mess for what feels like hours. I cry until I'm dehydrated and there are no more tears to cry. I cry until the stress of the entire situation is finally released and I am no longer holding it in. I cry for Byson. I cry for him having to marry Gabrielle. I cry for his mom and dad even though this is all his father's fault. I cry for me, my job, and my broken heart. I cry for the life I got to dream of if only for a single moment. And I cry for shattered promises.

I know Gabrielle's threats weren't idle and she will do whatever it takes to get her way. So, for now I will play her game. I will stay away from Byson. I will quietly leave my job at Taylor, Johnson, and Thayer Law Firm. All while silently trying to save him from her. She may do whatever it takes to get a man that doesn't even want her, but I will do whatever it takes to save the man I love.

With my resolve newly restored, I stand up, dry my face and make a vow that no matter what Gabrielle will not win.

****

When I finally turn my phone back on there were several missed calls and texts from Halle. I instantly text her back.

Sorry for the cold shoulder. I just needed time to clear my head.
OMG! She is such a bitch.
I know.
Me and Andrew are already on our way over. We have pizza, ice cream and wine.
Sys!
Sy!

I'm not really in the mood for company but staying home alone is also not something I want right now either. So, wanted or not, I welcome them both. Especially when they come bearing gifts like pizza and wine.

It's not long before they show up and envelop me in hugs. Andrew hits me with sad eyes and I want to cry all over again. Thankfully Halle breaks the sadness in the room, "Okay. Start from the beginning and tell us everything that bitch said to you today." I did. I told them everything. I even told them about her sticking her fingers in my pussy. By the time I was done telling them everything, both of them sat looking at me with their mouths gaping open. "Holy shit," Halle said.

"What even is your life?" Andrew asked.

"Honestly, I don't even know."

"Okay, so wait…" Andrew gets up and paces back and forth for a few minutes while Halle and I watch him. He suddenly stops, turns and looks at us and pops down onto the floor in front of us before saying, "So this bitch is making Mr. Thayer marry her for something his father did?"

"Yes," I say trying to figure out where he is going with this.

"He doesn't want to be with her?"

"No."

"He wants to be with you?"

"Yes."

"And you are sure about this?"

"Yes. Why?"

"What if I told you that I may have a way to help you?"

"What? How?" I ask excitedly.

"I have some connections that may be able to help find the information you are looking for."

"What connections?"

"It's better if you don't ask. Just send me their names and I'll get my people right on it."

"Well don't you sound all mob-like?" Halle teases while I send him the information. "With that settled, that bitch can't just make you quit," Halle snaps.

"She can and she did. I'm not going to let her ruin Byson's reputation. I won't let that happen."

"What is it about this man that you are willing to give up your career for him?"

"I'm not giving up my career. I'm only giving up one job. There will be plenty of other jobs."

Finally feeling like a weight has been lifted, I decided to get through the weekend and on Monday I would look for a new job.

23

I woke up this morning with my head held high, knowing deep in my heart I would land another job. I may have given up my dream job to protect the man I love, but I'm not going to let that stop me from moving forward. I dressed in my best professional blazer and slacks. I curled my hair and applied a subtle amount of makeup. I took one last look at myself in the mirror and approved of how professional I looked. I smiled at myself just for a little confidence, and headed out the door. I haven't had to look for a new job in a few years and to say I am nervous is an understatement.

I have turned my resume into several different law firms this morning. When I tried to speak to any of the hiring managers at the firms, they all seemed to have blown me off. Frustrated, I have decided to stop and grab some lunch before continuing my search.

I decided on Paulino's. Some good Italian food is always good for the soul even if the meal is heavy. When the hostess sat me, I heard someone call my name.

"Bellamy Adams? I haven't seen you since law school."

"Scarlett. Wow. Has it been that long?" I went to law school with Scarlett. We shared a dorm for our first two years at Harvard.

"Join me for lunch," she said, waving me over.

"Are you sure?"

"Of course I am. We have some catching up to do." I happily took my seat at Scarlett's table. The hostess looked pleased with the change as well. "So, tell me, what's new with you?"

"Not much is new. What about you? Did you and Stanley get married?"

"God, no. We split right after graduation. He wanted to explore as many women's land down under as possible while I was ready to start the next phase in our life."

"I'm so sorry to hear that."

"I'm not. Had he not cheated on me with twelve different women I would have never left him and would have never met my husband, Travis."

"Oh. How long have you been married?"

"Three years this December."

"That's amazing. Congratulations. Any kids?"

"Not yet. I just landed a partnership at the firm that I am currently at, so we plan to start trying soon."

"That is awesome. Where are you working?"

"Bailey, Simpson, and, well now, Smith," she said smiling so proudly. I couldn't help the little jealousy monster that wanted to rear its ugly little head.

"You wouldn't be in the market for a lawyer, would you?" I asked, feeling ashamed to have to even ask.

"Are you not currently working?"

"Not as of this past Friday."

"What happened?" she asked inquisitively.

"It's a long story. It has nothing to do with my performance or how I am as a lawyer."

"Okay. Let me get your information and I will see what I can do."

"Thanks, Scarlett."

"Any time girl. You helped me so much to get through my classes. I would have never passed if it weren't for you. It's time for me to return the favor."

Feeling like a huge weight had been lifted off my shoulders, we sat and caught up for the rest of our lunch. By the time it was over I was feeling really hopeful that I just landed a job at Bailey, Simpson, and Smith.

Leaving, Scarlett said, "I'll call you later this afternoon to let you know what we've got for you."

"Thanks again. It was so good catching up. Don't be a stranger."

"I won't."

We parted ways and I continued to drop my resume off at a few more law offices before heading home for the day. I figured it wouldn't hurt to have a few more resumes out there in case things didn't work out with Scarlett's firm.

I was just walking in the door of my apartment when my phone started ringing. It was Scarlett already calling me. My belly filled with excitement at the possibility of already having a job lined up. "Hello," I answered with more excitement in my voice than I meant to have.

"Hey, Bellamy. I just talked to my partners, and we need to talk."

"Okay. What's up?"

"I just talked to my partners about you and apparently they got a call about you already first thing this morning."

"Okay. Is that good or bad?" I ask, a little confused.

"It's bad, Bellamy. You have been blackballed. No one in this town, hell, in this state, will hire you. I don't know who you pissed off, but there was nothing I could do or say to convince them. They won't hire you, Bellamy. I'm sorry."

"Blackballed? Are you serious?"

"Yeah. I am so sorry."

"Okay. Thank you for letting me know, Scarlett."

"No problem honey. I hope everything works out for you."

"Somehow, I don't think that will be happening anytime soon." There was an awkward silence, neither of us knowing what to say, so I hurried off the phone. "Thanks again for trying. I'll talk to you later."

"Okay. Keep in touch, Bellamy." Somehow, her *keep in touch* didn't seem as genuine as when we were at the restaurant. I knew this would be the last time I would hear from Scarlett. She couldn't be associated with someone that has been blackballed. Even if I am wrongfully accused.

I pulled out my phone and texted Halle…

I've been fucking blackballed.

That fucking bitch!!! Want me to come over after work?

No. I think I'm going to get out of town for a few days. Maybe go to my brothers.

Okay. Just remember I'm here if you need me.

Thanks Halle.

Love you girl.

Love you too.

I decided getting away and clearing my head was exactly what I needed to do so I texted my brother to see if I could come for a visit.

Some shit has happened. Don't want to explain right now. Can I come for a visit?

His response came quicker than I expected.

Of course, you can. I'm out of town until the end of the week but come on up. You know where the key is. Let yourself in. Make yourself at home.

Thanks Mav. I'll head up tonight. See you this weekend.

Be careful. Let me know when you arrive.

With that settled, I grabbed my suitcase and started packing. There's nothing like a good getaway to help heal my shattered pieces.

24

The drive up to my brothers was long but peaceful. It's the time of year when summer is just starting to turn into fall and the leaves are changing colors. It is my favorite time of year. I love to see the different colors of the leaves that the trees produce. It's also another reason why I love to visit my brother's cabin this time of year. His cabin is nestled deep into the woods and is surrounded by the most beautiful trees. When I visit, we usually spend most of our day sitting out on the porch admiring the beautiful nature that surrounds his cabin.

When I get to my brother's cabin it is already dark which causes me to struggle to find the key to let myself in. Once I do manage to find it, I go inside and inhale the sweet smell of cedar. The scent instantly fills me with warmth and a sense of home.

Our parents died right after Mav turned twenty-two. Instead of letting me go into foster care at seventeen, he decided to step up and take me in. For the longest time we lived in a very small one bedroom apartment in the city. It was very important to him for me to finish high school and to go on to college. He worked nights while he put himself through the police academy. He didn't have plans to become a police officer that young but having to take care of me changed things a bit for him.

I try to visit him as much as I can, but both of our lives are hectic.

I get settled into his spare room that I always use when I visit and pull my e-Reader from my bag. I spent the next few hours getting lost in a book. It has been so long since I have had the time to pick up a book and read. It feels good to get lost in the pages of another reality because mine sure as hell isn't one I want to be in right now.

****

I must have fallen asleep reading last night. I was tired when I got here but I didn't think I was that tired. I decided on a shower first, then I would text Mav and Halle and let them both know that I made it okay.

I turned the water on as hot as it could go and let it steam up the bathroom before getting in. I stood under the spray of hot water and hoped it would wash away all of my troubles. I prayed the hot water would wash away everything wrong in my life right now. Byson wouldn't be marrying another woman. I wouldn't be blackballed. I wouldn't be jobless. I didn't know I was crying until a sob broke free from my chest. I was crying for Byson. For him being forced to marry someone he didn't want to be with. I was crying for me, for not being able to be with Byson and for having to leave my dream job. I was crying for the love we would never be able to share unless I could somehow find him a way out of this. But how? How could someone like me save him from someone like her and her father?

By the time my tears had dried, the water had turned cold. I got out and dried off. I threw my hair into a bun on the top of my head, not bothering to dry it. I grabbed a pair of leggings and a light sweater. It wasn't cold yet, but the temperature is dropping a little. Plus, I just want to be comfortable today. I grabbed my phone and shot the same message to Halle and Mav.

Made it safely.
Halle: Thank God. I was so worried when I didn't hear from you last night.
Mav: Good to hear. Got an early release. I'll be home tomorrow.

I decided to respond to Halle first.

Sorry. It was late when I got here, and I fell asleep. How long are you staying?
I don't know yet. Couple days, maybe a few more. How's Mav (wink, wink)

He will be home tomorrow.
Give him kisses for me lol
Sure thing Halle lol

She has had a major crush on my brother since she met him last year when she came with me for Thanksgiving. I think they would be perfect for each other but when she was here, he didn't seem to even notice her so I'm not sure he is even interested in her.

Once I was done texting Halle, I messaged Mav.

You don't have to come home early on my account. I'll be fine until the weekend.
You drive up suddenly without warning and you think I don't know something hasn't happened. I'm coming home, Bells. You obviously need me, or you wouldn't be at my house right now.
I love you.
I love you too. I'll see you tomorrow.

I don't know how he knows that I need him, but I guess that's why he's the big brother. Maybe there is just something built inside of older siblings that makes them automatically aware when something is wrong. Maybe it's just because we are so close even though we don't get to visit as much as we would like to.

With not much else to do, I grabbed my e-Reader, a cup of coffee and headed for the porch. If I can't work right now, I am going to make the most of my mini-vacation and relax as much as I can until I figure out what I am going to do about a job.

25

I tossed and turned all night. I barely got any sleep and what sleep I did get was filled with dreams of Byson. When I finally woke up for the day I felt like shit. My head was pounding and nausea washed over me. I got up and ran to the bathroom praying I would make it in time. I missed dinner last night, not because I wasn't hungry, but because I couldn't put my book down long enough to make myself something to eat, so there was nothing in my stomach to throw up but stomach acid. It burned the back of my throat causing me to gag. The bitter taste filled my mouth causing me to throw up even more.

Once there was nothing left, not even stomach acid, I grabbed a rag and wet it with cold water. I laid the rag on the back of my neck and let the coolness calm me a little. Once I was feeling a little better, I brushed my teeth and washed my face with cold water. I climbed back into bed and grabbed my phone. I immediately texted Halle.

I don't know what the hell is wrong with me, but my stomach seems to be the most sensitive thing on the planet lately.
What's wrong?
Just puked my guts up and still feel really nauseous.
Are you pregnant? :) JK

Her question threw me for a loop. There was no way I was pregnant. I had only slept with Byson. We didn't use a condom, but I am on birth control, and I never miss a pill. I tried calculating the date of my last period. For the life of me I can't remember.

Fuck!

There is no way.

My phone dinged, pulling me from my thoughts.

I was just joking, Bells.
Halle...
Oh fuck!
I have to go get a test.
I'm leaving right now. I'll be there in a couple of hours.
You don't have to do that. Mav will be home later.
I am on my way, Bells. This isn't something you will do alone. Wait for me and I will bring the test with me, and we can do this together.
Okay. Thank you.

Love you.
Love you too.

I can't be pregnant. How does this even happen? I mean I know how it happens but I'm on the pill. It has to be the flu. The lack of sleep from last night has left me unable to remember when my last period was correctly.

Right?

Sitting and waiting for Halle to show up for two hours is going to be the hardest thing I have ever had to do. All I can think about is the possibility of being pregnant. Could I really be pregnant? Every time I hear a car pass on the road, I run to the window thinking it's Halle pulling up. I was a nervous wreck and antsy by the time Halle finally showed up.

"I wasn't sure which test to get so I got three different ones," she announced as she walked through the door.

I took the test from her and went straight into the bathroom. I peed in the little cup that came with one of the tests. I opened all three of them and stuck them in the yellow-colored liquid. I held them there for the length of time required before pulling them out and recapping them. I laid them on the side of the bathtub, washed my hands, and walked out too afraid to look at the test.

"Well?" Halle asked as I walked into the living room.

"I don't know yet. We have to wait three minutes." I set the timer on my phone.

"How did this happen?" I looked at her as if she had lost her mind. "I know how this happens, Bells. I mean how did this happen to you? You are so responsible."

"I don't know. I'm on the pill. And yeah, like you said, I'm very responsible so I have never missed a pill."

"Maybe you just have the flu or something."

"I am hoping that's it." When the timer went off on my phone Halle and I both jumped. We looked at each other. I am too afraid to move. "I can't do it, Halle."

Halle got up to look at the test for me. I was too terrified to look for myself. When she came back out of the bathroom the look on her face told me all I needed to know. Tears burned the back of my eyes until they were flowing freely. Halle came over and sat beside me placing an arm around my shoulders. I laid my head on her arm and she let me cry. She held me for what felt like hours. She sat in silence supporting me the best way she knew how to.

Finally, after what felt like a lifetime of crying, the tears stopped. The fear was still there though. "What do I do?" I asked her.

"I don't know Bells. But I'm here for whatever you need."

"Who is the father? Is it Byson?"

"Yes."

"Are you going to tell him?"

"Do I have to?" I asked, already knowing the answer.

"Kind of."

"I know," I said letting out a huff. I know I have to tell him, obviously, but how do I do that? How do I tell the man that is marrying another woman that I am having his baby? How do I share a child with someone that I am in love with but can't be with?

I am so lost and so afraid.

How do I do this?

How do I make this work?

Of course, it's at this moment, when I have a tear stained face and puffy red eyes, that my very overprotective brother decides to walk in the front door. The anger that flashes across his face is indescribable. "What the fuck happened?" he asked with such malice I am almost afraid to answer him.

"Well, hello to you too," Halle says, trying to lighten the mood.

"What happened?" he asked again.

"You may want to go put your bag down, grab a beer from the fridge and get comfortable. We have a lot to catch you up on big brother," Halle says, answering for me. For whatever reason, he does what she says. I almost find it comical that he actually did what she told him to do.

Once he put his bag away, had his beer, and was seated in the chair across from us, we both filled him in on everything that has been happening. One of the reasons I came to see Mav in the first place is because he is a police officer, and he may be able to help me help Byson.

"You're in love?" he asked, sounding a little taken aback by the thought of it.

"Is that so hard to believe?" I ask, kind of offended.

"Well yeah considering you never had time for guys with your career." *Fair enough.* "And you're pregnant?"

"Yeah. I just took a test right before you got home."

"What are you going to do? Are you going to tell him?"

"Eventually. I want to try and get Gabrielle away from him first."

"Let me make a few calls and see what I can find out about them. The name sounds familiar, but I can't say I know for sure where from. It could take me a few days to find anything out."

"That's okay, we have nothing but time right now," Halle says, smiling at me.

"What about work?" I ask her as Mav goes off to make his calls.

"I have plenty of vacation time saved up. I called Myrtle on the way up to let her know I had a family emergency, and I wouldn't be in the rest of the week." Halle's phone started ringing. "Hang on a sec, it's Andrew."

"Who's Andrew?" Mav asked as Halle walked away to take the call.

"If I didn't know any better, I'd say you sound jealous."

"What? No. Just curious."

"Mm hmm," I say smiling at him. "Andrew is our friend who would be more interested in you than Halle, so no worries, he isn't into your girl. And just between the two of us, if you wanted to make a move, I know for a fact that Halle would be okay with it."

"And what about you? Would you be okay with that?"

"Are you kidding? Halle is amazing. She is my best friend and I think she would be perfect for you."

Halle came back into the room with a smile on her face. "That was Andrew, and his connections came through. He has some info on Gabrielle and her father but it is sensitive information so he wouldn't share it with me over the phone."

"So, I guess we have to go back to the city," I said, a little sad to leave.

"Not exactly," she said, causing both me and Mav to look at her. "I told him to come here. He is on his way."

"At this rate I should start charging a boarding fee since my home is turning into a hotel," Mav says.

"Oh hush. You know you enjoy having us here. It's not like you get this kind of company all the time," Halle says. "You are going to turn into a grumpy old man one day. Oh wait...who am I kidding. You already are a grumpy old man."

"I'm not old. I'm only thirty-three." Mav said, sounding offended.

"Oh, I'm sorry. The complaining you were doing made you sound older. Sorry, my bad," Halle said, causing me to laugh. She loved to aggravate him, and I think it is the funniest thing to watch.

"You girls hungry? I'll order us some pizza," he said changing the subject causing me and Halle to laugh even harder.

26

We ate pizza and talked, well I mostly watched Halle pick on Mav, while we waited for Andrew to get there. By the time he finally showed up it felt like an eternity had passed. I made quick introductions between Andrew and Mav and then Halle and I both said at the same time, "What did you find?"

"Geez ladies, can I at least get all the way in the door first before we start playing 20 questions?"

"Sorry." We both say in unison again.

Once Andrew gets to the couch, he makes a slow show of pulling out two files. He takes his sweet precious time and all I want to do is reach across the coffee table and snatch the files out of his hands. "What I am about to show you is very sensitive information and please don't ask me how I got the information. It isn't something we can legally use against them, and it isn't something that I obtained legally. Okay?"

"Okay." Me, Halle, and Mav answer. Andrew passes the files to me first. I take my time looking through the first one. By the time I'm done, I want to puke. There are pictures of murders in the file. There are pictures of, who I assume is, Adrian Delacroix beating a man. There are pictures of abused women and children, burning houses and businesses. Pictures of multiple people being tortured while Adrian stands there smiling, looking like he is enjoying the show. There are multiple police reports from women accusing him of rape and assault. There are also some from business owners claiming that Adrian has threatened them if they don't pay a business tax to him monthly. Once I'm done with the first, thicker file I pass it to whoever's hand was reaching out for it while I started looking through the other file.

This file didn't have as much in it. It was a file on Gabrielle. There were about fifty pictures of women who looked to be sex workers. I know it's illegal but nothing that's big time. Nothing that would give me enough ammo to get her away from Byson. There are a few police reports in this file as well. I pick up the first one and by the time I am done reading it, tears are freely falling from my eyes. The women in the pictures aren't women at all. They are girls, all under the age of sixteen. Gabrielle is into human trafficking. She is a worse human than I thought she was. I cannot let Byson marry her. But how do I use this information to my advantage?

I close the file and pass it to the next person.

No one says a word until Mav and Halle both have thoroughly gone through the files. It's Halle who speaks first. "Wow." she says blowing out a breath she probably didn't even know she was holding.

"Yeah. Wow," I say.

"What do we do now?" Andrew asks.

"I don't know yet," I say honestly. "I know legally we can't do anything with this information but maybe I can somehow present her with the information and scare her off. She doesn't need to know that we can't really do anything with it."

"Well, hang on." Mav says, causing the three of us to look over at him. "I know you got the information illegally, but I just got a text from one of my friends that works with the FBI. He says he is working on a case that involves the French mob and two people of interest are none other than Gabrielle and Adrian Delacroix. He doesn't live far from here. He will be here in thirty minutes."

"Holy shit. This just got interesting. We are going to need some popcorn for this shit show." Andrew said.

"Aren't you glad you came?" Halle asked him.

"Hell yeah. Who knew little Miss Responsible would get herself involved with the French mob?"

"Shut up," I snapped.

"Oh. Don't let her emotions bother you. That's just the pregnancy hormones," Halle said.

"Excuse me?" Andrew said, looking back and forth between Halle and me.

"Did I not mention that on the phone?" she asks.

"No, you most certainly did not."

"Found out this afternoon, hence why I'm here."

"This night just keeps getting spicier and spicier," Andrew says going into the kitchen and rummaging through the fridge for something to drink.

Andrew spent the next thirty minutes asking me questions about the baby. I didn't have many answers for him considering I just found out that I am pregnant. I was so thankful for the knock at the door when Mav's friend arrived so the subject could finally change.

Mav led his friend into the living room, only he isn't Mav's friend. He's my friend from school. "Tate?"

"Bellamy?" We both walked towards each other and embraced in what felt like the longest hug.

Maverick cleared his throat causing us to pull apart, "The two of you know each other?"

"We went to school together," I said studying Tate's face. He is a man now. There is no trace of the boy that I remember.

"College?" Mav asks"

"High school." Tate answers for me. "She was actually my prom date." He grabbed my hand and asked, "How have you been? Tell me everything."

"Can the reminiscing want until later? We have a job to do." Mav asked, seeming annoyed.

"Sorry," Tate said.

"Don't worry about the grumpy one. I'm Halle. This is Andrew," Halle said, taking Tate's hand and shaking it.

"Well, let's get started then, shall we?" Tate said, gesturing me towards the couch where he took a seat next to me.

Tate spent the next two hours going into full detail over everything we just read about Adrian and Gabrielle. It is way worse than the files could ever describe though. These are horrible people. Apparently, the FBI has been working on this case for almost three years. They have plenty of evidence but somehow, they can't get it to stick every time they try to make an arrest. They need a confession. And this is where I come into Tate's plan.

"No way. I'm not going to let her do that," Mav says standing up and pacing the floor.

"It's not your choice, Mav," I say.

"You can't be seriously thinking about doing this?"

"It's the only way."

"It can't be the only way."

"Listen Maverick, we will be there the whole time. We will make sure she is safe. We won't let anything happen to her," Tate says, trying to convince him.

"I have to do this, Mav. I have to protect Byson. Not only is he the man I love, but he is the father of my baby. I will ask for a meeting with Gabrielle. I will take the files Andrew brought, threaten her with them and try to coax a confession out of her. Trust me, she will talk. She likes to brag about herself and her father. I have to do this. I will do this with or without your blessing."

Mav lets out a sigh knowing there is no way he will win this fight and says, "Fine, but I will be there with you."

"She won't meet me with you there."

"I will be hiding Bells. I'll be right there beside Tate listening in on the whole thing. Right Tate?" he asks, daring him to deny him this request. Tate nods his head in agreement.

We go over the plan one more time and it feels like a little bit of the weight I have been carrying on my shoulders has lifted a bit. Exhaustion has taken over and suddenly I'm so tired I can hardly stand to keep my eyes open. I tell them all goodnight and let them know I will see them all in the morning.

27

When I woke up the smell of eggs and bacon sent me hurdling straight into the bathroom. The pizza from last night making a reappearance as everything in my stomach empties into the toilet. How will I ever make it through this pregnancy if I keep throwing up like this? How far along am I? I need to call a doctor and set up an appointment. I add that to my mental checklist of things I need to get done today. One of those things being to call and set up a meeting with Gabrielle. I'll have to call Myrtle for that and that is a call I'm dreading. She will have a ton of questions for me as to why I quit like I did. And I can't give her any answers.

Maybe I'll have Halle call her and do it for me. That thought makes me giggle to myself cause Halle hates talking to Myrtle more than anyone does. As much as Halle loves me and will do anything for me, she will hate to do this.

Once my stomach is settled enough to move around, I jump in the shower and quickly wash up before heading down to meet with the others.

When I finally get downstairs, everyone is sitting at the table eating the bacon and eggs that just caused me to vomit. I grab a pack of crackers from the cabinet and a ginger ale from the fridge and sit down next to Halle and put my head on her shoulder.

"Morning sickness?" she asks, laying her head on top of mine. I nod my head letting her know that is in fact exactly what it is. "Poor thing," she says. "But I'm glad it's you and not me."

"Ugh, thanks," I say lifting my head up.

"I have informed my boss of the plan and we are good to go when you can set up a meeting with Gabrielle," Tate says.

"Oh, that reminds me," I say looking over at Halle. "Will you call Myrtle for me and have her set the meeting up?" She instantly says no before letting me explain. "If I call her, she will have a million questions about why I quit."

"Maybe you shouldn't have quit," she snaps.

"You know I didn't have a choice. Please Halle? Do this for me?"

"Ugh, fine. But you are going to owe me big time for this."

"Thank you."

When she goes off to call Myrtle, I get a ping on my phone letting me know I have a new text message. My heart sinks to the pit of my stomach when I see who its from....Byson.

You up and quit. Halle and Andrew have taken the week off. What's going on Bellamy?

You shouldn't be messaging me Byson.

Why are the three of you missing work? What is going on?

I can't tell you right now and again, we shouldn't be talking.

So, something is going on then?

Byson, please.

I'm worried about you. Why can't you talk to me? I miss you.

Tears sting the backs of my eyes at his message. I don't respond though. I can't. Not yet. I miss him so much it hurts to even think about it. I want nothing more than to run to him and wrap my arms around him and tell him everything. I want to tell him about Gabrielle's threat to me. How she forced me to quit. How she had me blackballed. I want to tell him what a horrible person she is and tell him not to marry her. But I know it would all be for nothing. He has no choice but to marry her in his eyes. It is the only way to save his mother and father.

I hate his father for doing this to him. I hate Gabrielle for making her father do this to him. And I hate Andrian Delacroix for letting Gabrielle make him let her do this to him on behalf of his own father.

Who knew I had so much room in my heart for this much hate?

Halle came back into the kitchen pulling me from my thoughts. "Myrtle said she will call me later with confirmation if Gabrielle agrees to the meeting or not."

We decided last night that I would meet Gabrielle at my apartment since there couldn't be people around and meeting at an abandoned warehouse or empty parking lot would be too suspicious. Plus, they only do that kind of thing in movies or books. Tate said his boss had guys go in this morning and set up hidden cameras in my apartment. The thought of strange people I don't know going into my apartment messing around with my things weirds me out, but I keep reminding myself that this is for the greater good. Tate said they also have secured the apartment that is across the hall from mine for them to hide out in while she is at my apartment. That is if she takes the bait.

It hasn't even been ten minutes since Halle returned to the kitchen and her phone started ringing. "Hello," she says. "Okay. Sounds good. I will let her know." Halle hung up her phone and looked at me and smiled. "She took the bait. The meeting is at seven."

I don't know why I suddenly got so nervous. I want to do this so badly, but nerves in the pit of my stomach are making me have second thoughts. Not that I would back out. Especially not now that she has agreed to meet with me. But, still, I feel like a nervous wreck.

"We will need to head back to the city soon, so we have time to set up and make sure everything is working correctly," Tate says getting up from the table. And with that we all got up and got ready to leave.

28

By the time we reached my apartment my nerves had settled down a little bit. I'm still nervous, but now I feel more like an Avenger going on a mission than a small human about to take on the head of the French Mob's daughter. Tate and Maverick got to work on making sure all of the equipment that the guys set up earlier is working properly. They made me go into my bedroom while they checked all of the cameras because they didn't want me to know where they were hidden so I wouldn't subconsciously look at them while talking to Gabrielle.

Once all of the equipment was all checked, they let me come out only to ask me if I was comfortable wearing a wire. "No. I can't wear that."

"Why not?" Mav asks, folding his arms across his shoulders.

"What if she notices? What if she checks? What if I do something by accident to let her know that I am

184

wearing a wire? All of this would be for nothing, so no. I will not wear a wire. There are plenty of cameras in here, I'm sure."

"What about an earpiece?" Mav asks.

"No. She could see it."

"Still as stubborn as always," Tate says, smiling at me.

"Some things never change," I say, smiling back.

"It's almost seven. We need to head across the hall in case she shows up a few minutes early."

I let out a breath I didn't even know I was holding as I watch Tate, Mav, Halle, and Andrew leave my apartment to face this monster semi-alone.

I pace back and forth across my living room floor for twenty minutes, certain I was wearing a hole in the carpet when there was finally a knock at my door. I straightened my hair out and dusted the nothingness that was on my clothes off before I opened the door.

"Gabrielle, thank you for coming on such short notice."

"Bellamy. Nice to see you again," she said, pasting on a fake smile.

"Come in please," I say moving out of her way and letting her walk inside. "Can I get you anything to drink?" I offer.

"No thanks." She takes a seat on the couch and looks at me with a pointed stair. "What is this little meeting all about Bellamy? I thought I made myself clear."

"I have an offer for you."

She laughs and it makes me want to stab her in the throat. So much hate for this woman. "What offer could you possibly make me?"

"I want you to leave Byson. Don't marry him."

"And why exactly would I agree to that?"

"Because if you don't agree to it, I will go to the FBI and give them all of the information that I have on you and your father."

Oh yeah, and what information would that be?"

I get up and grab the files that I left sitting on the kitchen counter. I bring them to her and drop them on the coffee table in front of her. "This information."

She picks up the files and studies both of them and I study her. Only once does she let her composure slip, but within seconds it is right back in place. Once she is done looking at the files, she stuffs them into her purse and says, "Well, first of all, no one will believe you. Second of all, I will be taking these with me. You do understand, don't you? I can't have these fall into the wrong hands now, can I?"

"If you think those are my only copies, then you are sadly mistaken. I will only make this offer once. Leave Byson. Go back to France. Call off the wedding and forget you ever knew him."

"You really love him, don't you?"

"Yes, I do."

"You want to marry him."

"Yes.

"You will do anything for him."

"Yes."

"Ah, that is sweet. Being in love is sweet. Loving someone so unconditionally is so sweet. But this has nothing to do with you and everything to do with me. I told you that I love Byson too. That I have been in love with him for years. Byson is mine and he will always be mine. These idle threats that you are so cutely trying to make mean nothing to me. Do you know who I am? You have seen the evidence for yourself. And if you don't want to find yourself on the wrong side of the evidence, you will be the one that forgets Byson."

"Is that a threat? What? You will have me killed if I don't disappear?"

"Something like that?"

"Is that what happens to the underaged girls that try to escape when you pimp them out?"

She laughs again but this time there is so much malice behind it that it sounds more like a cackle. "Those girls should be thankful for me. I take them from shitty homes, abusive parents, homes without food, water, or heat. I give them food. I give them clothes. I give them running water. I give them a roof over their heads that's not a rotting shithole."

"And all they have to do in return is have sex with grown men, right?" I ask, cutting her off.

"That's right. The cost of sex is nothing compared to what I do for these girls. They should be thankful."

"And what about the men your father tortures and kills? Should they be so thankful too? What about the businesses he burns down when someone doesn't pay him his business taxes? Should they be so thankful too?"

"They should all be so thankful. Things could have been much worse for those people my father tortured and killed. And as far as the businesses he burned down, those people got their insurance money, yeah, my father got his cut, but they got something out of it too. So, yes, they should all be so thankful."

"You and your father are monsters. And I will do whatever it takes to stop Byson from marrying you."

"That will never happen."

"Get out of my apartment," I growl unable to look at her another minute.

"This is the last meeting we will have, Bellamy." Before she walks out the door she turns around and looks at me and says, "Oh, and if I were you, I'd watch my back."

29

Once she was gone for about ten minutes, Halle, Mav, Andrew, and Tate came rushing into my apartment. Mav pulled me into a hug and said, "You did such a good job. I'm so proud of you, sis."

"Thanks." I didn't feel proud though. I felt disgusting and dirty. I felt like I had Gabrielle's filth all over me even though she never touched me. Just being in the same room as that monster made me feel like I was an accomplice to all of her criminal activities.

"I wish you would have cunt punched her," Halle said, causing everyone to look at her with raised eyebrows. "What?" she asked innocently. "I'm not the only one thinking it. I'm just the only one willing to say it out loud."

I couldn't help but laugh at her. This is why I love her. It is because of moments like this when I am feeling like shit, she knows how to make me laugh without even knowing that she needs to.

"Mother fucker." Tate says in frustration.

"What's wrong?" I ask.

"Nothing recorded."

"What?"

"The cameras didn't record. We didn't get any of that."

"You're joking, right?"

"I wish I was, but no, I'm not."

I flop down on the couch defeated. This was our one and only chance to try and scare her away from Byson. How do we get her away from him now? Not only did she take the files with her, but now we don't have a single shred of evidence of her confessing to everything she just confessed to.

This can't be how it ends.

Frustration builds up inside of me and I start to feel claustrophobic. There are too many people in my apartment. There is too much noise around me. I need out. I need air. I know they won't let me leave here alone. I grab my phone and go into my bedroom and shut and lock the door. I open my window and go down the fire escape. It is the only way I will be able to get out alone. I need to clear my head. I need to think. I need to come up with another plan. And I can't do that surrounded by them right now. Once I'm a few blocks away, I text Halle to let her know I went for a walk but told her I went in the opposite direction just in case they come looking for me.

I was almost five blocks away when I see a black SUV creeping up beside me. At first, I think it could be Byson, but then the back window rolls down and a guy with brown hair sticks his arm out of the window and points a gun at me. I don't have time to react before the gun goes off.

I hear five shots.

I feel the pain spread all over my body. I smell the gunpowder as it lingers in the air and permeates my nose. I feel the warmth of the blood as it seeps from the bullet holes. Then I feel the cold ground. I smell the dirt that my face fell into. I feel the grass as it tickles my cheeks and nose. I can't see anything but a wad of chewed up gum that someone spit out and I think this is an odd thing to be thinking about when I'm lying here dying. Shouldn't my life be flashing before my eyes?

I hear the tires screech on the pavement as they pull off leaving me to die alone on the side of the road. My vision is becoming dark. I'm fading fast. I'm losing too much blood. I can hear the pounding of footsteps though. Someone is running towards me. I hear someone screaming out my name. I feel warm hands on my body as someone turns me over.

"Bellamy! Oh God, Bellamy! Stay with me. Call 911." The person holding me yells to someone behind him. "Stay with me, Bells. Don't die on me. Please don't die."

"Mav?"

"I'm here, Bells. Stay with me."

"I...l...l....love...y...you."

"No dammit. NO! BELLAMY!"

****

Beep. Beep. Beep. Beep. Beep.

There is a pestering, repeating beeping in my head that is driving me crazy. The smell of alcohol and sterilization fills my nose and takes over my senses. I try to move my arm but pain shoots through my entire body at the motion and I cry out.

"Bellamy?" I hear Mav's voice, but I can't see his face yet. I try to open my eyes, but the task is so hard. My eyelids feel like they have one hundred pound weights on them. After a few tries, I finally get them open. The lights in the room are dim, making it hard to see Mav's face.

"I'll go get the doctor," I hear Halle say.

"Water?" My mouth feels like I have licked the bottom of the Sierra desert. Mav helps me get a drink of water and when I've had enough, I ask, "What happened?"

"You were shot, Bells."

"Shot?"

"Yeah. You have been in a coma for over a week now."

I suddenly remembered the black SUV that pulled up beside me and I can clearly see the man with the dark hair that pulled out the gun. I remember the sound of the gunshots and the smell of the gunpowder. Tears start to freely fall from my eyes as I remember what happened to me. Then I suddenly remember the most important thing and panic fills me. "The baby, Mav. What about the baby?"

"You were shot in your left shoulder and your right arm. You were grazed on the left side of your neck and right on the top of your head. The last shot missed you completely. You have had two surgeries on your left shoulder already and you need one more on your right arm." He is avoiding the question.

"I don't care about that, Mav. What about the baby? Is the baby, okay?"

"The baby is fine for now. You have lost a lot of blood and there is still a chance that you may lose the baby, but for now the baby is fine."

I let out a breath of relief. Thank God my baby is okay. Halle comes back in with a man in a white coat following behind her. She walks over to Mav and stands behind him and places her hand on his shoulder. I make a mental note to ask them about that later.

"Good evening, Ms. Adams. How are you feeling?"

"Like a shit sandwich that has been chewed up and spit out."

"Have you been told what happened to you?"

"Unfortunately."

"We have the surgery scheduled for your right arm in the morning. It will be a very quick surgery as long as all goes well. You are on the right road to a very good recovery. By next week you will start physical therapy."

"When can I go home?"

"As long as the surgery goes well, I don't see why you can't go home the day after that."

"Mav said there is a possibility that I could still lose my baby?"

"With any injury as severe as yours there is always a possibility. And there is even a bigger risk when surgery is involved."

"What if I don't want the surgery?"

"I recommend you have the surgery."

"What is it for?"

"We found a small tear in one of your nerves and we just need to go in and repair it. It is something we missed in the initial surgery when we removed the bullet."

"And what happens if I don't get the surgery?"

"You could be facing a lot of future pain in your arm."

"So potential pain in my arm for the rest of life or risk to the life of my unborn child. Sorry doc, but I choose my child. I don't want the surgery."

"Ms. Adams…"

"Bells…"

Mav and the doctor try to convince me at the same time, but I cut them both off. "No. I don't want the surgery at the potential cost of my child."

"As you wish. In that case, you can go home tomorrow. I want to keep you overnight for observation just to make sure everything is okay. Just make sure you get plenty of rest today."

"That I can agree too." The doctor turned to leave but I stopped him just before we walked out the door. "Hey doc, how far along am I?"

"Twelve weeks."

Twelve weeks? That's three months. That would mean that I got pregnant almost the first time Byson and I slept together. I rub my hand over my stomach and feel the tiny bump that is starting to grow, and I'm instantly filled with so much love for this child growing inside of me, for this child I haven't even met yet. The thought is unfathomable.

30

I'll run Halle to your apartment to grab you some clothes for the ride home tomorrow," Mav says. "I also want to grab a shower and some food. Will you be okay for a couple hours while we do that?"

"I'll be fine, Mav. I'm tired. I'll just sleep while you're gone."

Halle walks up beside the bed and carefully sits beside me and says, "I am so glad you are okay, Bells. I was so afraid we were going to lose you."

"I'm fine, Hals," I say taking her hand in mine and giving it a small squeeze.

Once they leave, I want nothing more than to fall asleep. Even though I have been in a coma for the past week. I am about to doze off when I hear the door slowly creak open. Dreading having to deal with whatever nurse just interrupted me, I slowly open my eyes.

"Ah good, you're awake."

"What are you doing here?"

Gabrielle pulled off her coat and threw it on the chair beside my bed before taking a seat on the edge of it. "I had to come see for myself that you actually survived. I guess it is true what they say."

"And what would that be?"

"That if you want something done right you have to do it yourself."

Realization filled me as I understood what she was saying. "You did this?"

"I didn't technically pull the trigger but yes, I hired the idiots to kill you. I should have known that hiring some random wanna-be thugs off the street for a last minute job wouldn't get the job done. But desperate times call for desperate measures."

"Why did you try to have me killed?"

"Isn't it obvious? I want Byson. Byson wants you. You want me gone and threatened to turn me and my father over to the FBI. I have to get rid of you, Bellamy."

"So, this isn't over? You still plan on trying to kill me?"

"That's why I'm here, isn't it? I didn't think your brother and his little girlfriend would ever leave. Watching the two of them cozying up in the hallway is sickening." I watch her as she pulls something out of her coat pocket. She puts it in front of her face and checks the dosage. It's a syringe filled with a clear liquid.

"What is that?"

"This is an untraceable drug that will unmistakably..." Gabrielle is cut off by the door opening. She rushes to shove the syringe back into her pocket before she can get caught with it.

"What are you doing here?" Byson asked her.

"I am just checking up on your most valued employee. As soon as I heard about what happened I rushed right over to check on her," she says playing innocent. "What are you doing here?"

"The same thing." He also tries to act like he is only there to check on an employee. I can see the worry and the sadness in his eyes though.

I want Gabrielle to leave so I can have Byson to myself. I want him to lay with me on the bed and hold me, tell me everything is going to be okay. I want to tell him about the baby and about how much I love him and how I never want to go another day without showing him just how much love I have for him.

I look between the two of them. Gabrielle is studying Byson and Byson is studying me. What I would give for a doctor or a nurse to come into the room right now to break the tension. Instead, Byson pulls up a chair on the other side of my bed and sits next to me.

"Has the doctor said anything about recovery to you yet?" he asks.

I don't really want to give any information away in front of Gabrielle, so I decide to lie. "He says I have to stay in the hospital for a few more days. Possibly another week for observation."

"I know they were talking about another surgery, any news on when that will be?"

Another surgery? Had he been here before today? "Not having it," I say.

"Why not? Isn't it an important surgery?"

"I don't want it," I say matter of fact. Sensing that I don't want to talk about it, he drops the subject. The tension in the room is so thick you can cut it with a knife, and it is starting to make me feel extremely uncomfortable.

"Gabrielle, would you mind giving me a few minutes alone with Bellamy?"

"But I came…"

"Gabrielle, just a few minutes. Please." The tone in his voice told her it was a command, not a request. She grabbed her coat and left the room. When the door closed behind her, I let out an exasperated breath. He got up and sat next to me on the bed. "Tell me why you quit the firm Bellamy."

"I'm not doing this right now, Byson."

"Why won't you give me any answers?" He stands up and starts pacing back and forth at the foot of the bed. "You quit without any warning. No goodbye. Nothing. And now you won't explain why. Something is going on with you baby and I don't understand why you won't let me help you." The sound of hearing him call me baby filled my body with a heat I didn't know I missed.

"You can't help me with this, Byson."

He runs his fingers down his face almost looking defeated. "Why not?"

"You just have to trust me."

"It is killing me to know that there is something so big that you are going through that it almost cost you your life and you won't let me help you."

"Don't marry her," I blurt out.

"What?"

"Don't marry her."

"I have to Bellamy. I have to for my mom. If I had a choice I wouldn't, but you know I don't have a choice."

"I know." I sound just about as defeated as he looks. "Come here." He comes over and sits on the bed next to me. "I know I shouldn't be, but right now I want to be selfish. Will you hold me for a few minutes?"

"I would love to do nothing more than to hold you right now, baby." He slides in next to me, wraps his arm around my shoulders and pulls me into his chest. "I have missed you so much."

"I have missed you too, Byson." I close my eyes and take in the scent of him and log it to memory. If I can't find another way to save him, I want to be able to remember everything about this moment.

"Bellamy."

"Yeah."

"I love you. I have been in love with you for a long time now."

"Don't tell me that yet."

"But it's the truth."

"I know. But right now, if you marry her, it will only turn into a shattered promise, and I can't handle that right now."

"Okay. Can I be selfish for a minute too?"

"Yes."

"Can I kiss you?"

"Yes."

Byson kisses me so softly that I almost don't register that our lips have even touched at first. It's the heat from the kiss that ignites something inside of me. Suddenly, I'm kissing him harder, more passionately. I'm grabbing for him, needing him to be closer to me. He suddenly pulls away and leans his forehead against mine. Both of us are breathless.

"God, Bellamy."

"I know."

"I have to go. I don't think Gabrielle will wait out in the hall much longer."

He kisses me on the forehead before getting off the bed. He's almost to the door before I stop him, "Hey, Byson."

"Yeah."

"I'm getting released tomorrow so if you plan on coming back to the hospital I won't be here. I didn't want Gabrielle to know I would be going home." He nodded his understanding before turning and walking out the door leaving me alone to analyze everything that had just happened.

Gabrielle is the one responsible for trying to kill me and she is still hell bent on trying to make that happen.

Byson is in love with me and has been in love with me for quite some time now.

How do I get rid of the woman that is trying to kill me while trying to save the man I love from her?

31

After what felt like only a few minutes of sleep, the door to my hospital room flies open jumping me out of my sleep. "What the hell?" I yell.

"Sorry," Halle says.

"Are you okay?" Mav asks, looking as if he has seen a ghost.

"Yes. Why?"

"We got it, Bells. We got everything," he says smiling.

"You got what?" I ask, more than a little confused.

"Tate had the brilliant idea to put hidden cameras in your hospital room in case whoever tried to kill you decided to come back. And we got Gabrielle confessing to hiring the guys to kill you and we have her admitting to wanting to kill you again with the syringe. We got it. And no fuck ups this time."

"We got it?"

"We got it."

I felt like a weight had been lifted off my shoulders. "What happens now?"

"Tate will take it from here. It will be a little while before they can make an arrest so you will have to hide out at my place until then. But it's over Bellamy."

I couldn't help the tears of relief, of joy, of happiness that fell from my eyes. It will all be over soon.

****

"Oh my god. Turn the TV on," Halle said, rushing into the living room.

"What is it?" Mav and I asked at the same time.

"Just hush and listen." She turned the volume up on the TV and the three of us stood there in silence as the woman spoke.

Just in. FBI agent Tate Winters is being deemed a local hero for his arrest of the head of the French Mob, Adrian Delacroix, and his daughter Gabrielle Delacroix. They were both arrested late last night. Mr. Delacroix was arrested for numerous counts of assault, torture, rape, and murder. Ms. Delacroix was arrested for sex trafficking and for the attempted murder of our very own Attorney at Law, Bellamy Adams. Agent Winters has been working on this case for almost three years when he had a break in the case when Ms. Delacroix had a failed attempt at hiring hitmen to murder Ms. Adams where she then attempted to kill Ms. Adams herself in her room of Madison University Hospital just a short two months ago. There was secret surveillance hidden in Ms. Adams' hospital room and they were able to catch Ms. Delacroix red-handed. Once caught, she wasn't going down alone. She was more than willing to turn her father in in order to try and cut a deal with the DA. We will have more on this story tonight at seven. I'm Whitney Farrell and this is WABX.

"Oh. Wow," I say falling back onto the couch.

"Bells, do you know what this means?"

"Halle."

"Bells. Call him."

At the same time, I reached for my phone, it started ringing.

"Byson," I say as soon as the phone is to my ear.

"Bellamy. It's time for me to be selfish again," he says.

"Okay."

There was a knock on the door and when I turned around Mav was already letting Byson inside. "How did you know where to find me?" I asked.

"Halle told me where you were last night after I reached out to her to try and find you once Gabrielle was arrested." I ran to Byson, and he caught me with open arms. "Did you know about her?" he asked.

"Yes. I'm sorry I couldn't tell you. I was working with Tate to try and save you."

"You did that for me?"

"Yes. I would do anything for you."

"Is there anything else I should know about?"

"Yeah, there is one other thing." I grabbed Byson's hand and placed it on my now very prominent baby bump. He looked at me with wide eyes filled with not only shock but warmth and love.

When I told Byson about the baby, I was expecting him to be upset that I kept it from him, but he understood my reasoning.

"Bellamy."

"Yeah."

"I love you."

"I love you too."

Epilogue

One year later

Standing at the altar watching Halle walk down the aisle towards my brother is something I didn't think I would ever see but here we are. She looks absolutely beautiful, and I couldn't be happier to officially make her my sister. Apparently, my almost dying a year ago brought them together and they have been inseparable ever since. I can't complain though because the same can be said for me and Byson.

Ever since that day he walked into my brother's house he has never left my side. Even when our beautiful daughter, Sophie, was born seven months ago he was right there by my side the whole time I was yelling and cursing at him. We married within a couple of weeks after Gabrielle's arrest. We had a small ceremony in the Bahamas. We only invited close family and friends. Maverick walked me down the aisle and gave me away. It was perfect.

Byson offered me my job back at the law firm but since having Sophie I haven't had the desire to work. I want to spend all of my time with her. I don't want to miss out on a single first of hers.

Adrian Delacroix was sentenced to federal prison for life. He will never see the light of day again. Same can't be said for Gabrielle. She started her sentence in an women's prison until she tried reaching out to Byson once. When he told her that he didn't want anything to do with me and that we were happily married and had a child she lost her shit. She had to be moved to a psychiatric facility. She will spend the remainder of her life sentence in the psych ward.

As for Byson's parents, his father has been cut off by Byson and his mother. Byson is currently helping her file for divorce. Doing what he did to Byson and his mother is unforgivable and I don't blame either of them for cutting him off. I would have done the same thing.

His mother has moved closer to us so she can be near Sophie. She also welcomed me with open arms. She treats me like a daughter and if I'm being honest, I see her as a mother. No one will ever replace my mother, but going through life without mine for all this time makes me appreciate my mother-in-law even more. Not to mention, she has also taken Mav in as well and she treats him like a son. Byson and Mav act just like brothers and they get along so well. I have the picture perfect family and I couldn't ask for anything more.

I can honestly say our story ended with a happily ever after.

Extras

Want more? Check out the first chapter of *Corruption of the Heart* by Jessica Manson.

Chapter One

L iving in a world with no friends can be very lonely and very hard. I watch people around my school and how they all have friends. I see how they interact with one another and I long for the same interactions; I long for friendship. I distance myself from everyone around me by burying myself in my studies. When my head isn't in a book, I plug in my headphones and tune everyone out around me.

My parents died three months ago in a car accident leaving me to live with an aunt I've never met, in Maine. In my life back in Mississippi, I had a ton of friends and would spend most of my time with them, but when my parents died the pain was too much. I decided to distance myself from everyone to keep my heart protected. And since I didn't have friends in this new town to help me cope, I found my own way of dealing with things. Distance from any and all people was my form of therapy.

So, since I moved to Maine and haven't tried to make any friends, by keeping to myself, people tend to stay away from me and give me my space. This is why I found it extremely odd when Ambi Oakleaf sat at the lunch table with me and tried to talk to me.

Ambi isn't one of the popular girls in school, but all of the girls envied her even if they never would admit it. She is beautiful, almost goddess like. She is very tall for a girl and skinny with legs that seem to just go on for miles. Her skin is caramel colored and seems to glisten when the light hits her just right. Everyone seemed to be intimidated by her. Her reputation labeled her as a person to be afraid of. It didn't help that she was a part of a group called the "Corrupt Ones". And because of that everyone stayed away from her. The "Corrupt Ones" are apparently a group of kids that hang out together that supposedly do bad and reckless things and they are labeled as the bad kids of the school. Although I don't understand why they are called that, I have never actually seen them do anything that would make them so corrupt. They tend to stay to themselves. The "Corrupt Ones" are made up of eight members including seven guys and one girl.

Surprisingly, one of the guys in the group has always seemed to stick out to me. He seemed like he didn't belong with the rest of them. His actions seemed to present him as being different to the rest. When the others from the group seemed to be playing around, he stayed focused and detached himself from the group. I don't want to say he seemed better than the others but maybe not as bad. It didn't help that I had a little crush on him.

Odin is beautiful in an angelic kind of way. He has the same caramel skin color as Ambi with jet black hair and a jaw line that seemed to be carved by an Egyptian god. He is astonishingly handsome. I do my best every day to be as discreet as possible and sneak in as many peeks of him that I can. I think all of the other girls in school feel the same way I do, but they would never have the nerves to actually date him. The girls around here care way too much about their image and would never be caught dead with one of the "Corrupt Ones".

The girls around this school seem to be more focused on their image than anything else. Even though they all think that all of the members of the group are very beautiful. They would never try to date any of them. They wouldn't even admit that they thought they were hot. Every single girl in this school definitely looks, but they would never ever touch.

This school is just like any other school. There isn't anything special or fancy about it. Nothing stands out except for the billions of different smells radiating from so many students. The different types of perfumes, colognes, soaps, shampoos, and pets. The halls are dimly lit and smell dingy. The cafeteria is small and overcrowded. The only decent area in the school is the library.

"How's it going? Ambi asked me as if we were best friends and we talked every day.

Looking at her dumbfounded, I replied, "Okay, I guess."

Catching the questioning look on my face she introduced herself, "Hi, I'm Ambi Oak…"

Cutting her off I said, "I know who you are, I'm just wondering why you are sitting here, talking to me?" Realizing how rude I sounded I quickly tried to recover by saying, "I mean I don't mind if you sit here but why *are* you sitting here?"

"Well, I came over here today because I noticed that you always sit alone. We," she turned and pointed to the group of guys, "have been watching you since you started going to this school and we noticed that no one ever sits with you. You never even try to talk to anyone. We figured that at first it was because you are new here and that you just needed time to get used to things," she said, as she looked at me with wonder. "But it has been a few months and we can't seem to figure out why you don't make any friends with anyone. I mean, come on, even the lamest geekiest kids can make friends," she said, as she looked over to the table filled with the "geeky" kids.

I didn't know how to respond. I sat there looking at her pondering over everything she said before the realization of her words sunk in. Once I realized what she said, anger took over, "Wait, y'all have been watching me? Why?" Embarrassment took over as I realized that Odin had to have been watching me too.

"Doesn't really matter. Anyways Lilith, why do you stay to yourself so much?"

"Seriously?" I asked furiously. "You want me to tell you why I stay to myself? Have you ever thought that maybe everyone here is superficial and a waste of my time? *This* is a waste of my time and if you will excuse me, I have better things to do than to sit here and be interrogated by you. And who are you anyways? No one, so unless you want to answer me about why y'all have been watching me, I suggest you stay away from me."

"Like I said, it doesn't really matter."

"Then leave me alone." I knew I wasn't going to get any answers from her, so I gathered my things and stormed out of the lunchroom. I headed to the library to find a book to escape into for the remainder of my lunch period. As I made my way to the fiction section of the library, I noticed a shadow in my peripheral vision. I looked to my left to see Odin standing there with his back up against one of the bookshelves just inches from me, arms crossed and staring at me.

Heat flushed through my body when I noticed his beauty up close as he stood there. He has the most beautiful shimmering green eyes I have ever seen on anyone. They were almost emerald and if I allowed myself, I could definitely get lost in them. They were so green they almost glowed. This was the closest I have ever been to him and for the first time, I noticed his scent. He smelled so good like soap, sand, and ocean. Almost rustic but sweet at the same time.

I realized he was watching me with a smile on his face and embarrassment washed over me. I could feel my face get hot and turn red. I must have been staring at him like a googly-eyed crazy person. I wanted nothing more than for the floor to open up and swallow me up and take me away from this embarrassing moment.

"What do you want?" I snapped. When embarrassed, I either laugh so hard I can't breathe, or I get really mad and right now; I wasn't in the mood for laughter.

His eyebrows furrowed with uncertainty before he spoke. "I just want to apologize for the way Ambi acted back there. She can be very outspoken and matter of fact."

"You think?" I asked with an attitude I didn't recognize. "Apology not accepted. She told me how y'all have been watching me. And you know what? I think it is just downright creepy. Stay away from me Odin and stop watching me." I noticed a look of hurt wash over his face as I was about to storm off to find a place to be alone.

"So, you know my name?" he asked, causing me to turn around.

"What?" I asked, a little taken aback.

"I was just shocked that you know my name."

"Of course, I know your name. You are in a couple of my classes, and you do have to say here, when the teacher calls roll," I snapped.

"I was just saying it is nice to know that you actually know my name," he said, with a bit of sorrow in his voice before he walked off.

Feeling bad for hurting his feelings I just wanted to escape, but there wasn't a single place in the school where I could go and not be bothered. Students filled every inch of this place. I decided the best place to be alone around here would be in the comfort of my own car. It was a 1991 Mercedes. It was silver with a black leather interior. It wasn't much but it had been my parents and it was paid for. I decided to keep it when they died. My aunt tried to get me to sell it, but I figured I needed the car more than she needed the money from me selling it.

As I sat alone in my car, questions fled through my mind as I wondered what the "Corrupt Ones" wanted with me. Why were they talking to me now after all this time? I have been going to this school for almost three months and they just now want to talk to me? And why were they watching me? When were they watching me? At school? Home? Have they been following me? Panic took over and I needed to calm myself down.

At this moment, I wished I had friends, so I could have someone to talk to, someone I could feel safe with. Since I didn't have any friends, I did the next best thing to get my emotions under control. I reached inside the glove compartment and grabbed the razor blade I had hidden. I rolled up my sleeve and pulled the blade across my skin until I felt the pain escape my open flesh. I sat there watching the blood drip down from my arm and the calm started to take over.

I sat there in my own little world of ecstasy debating if I should go home for the day or stay in this asinine school. As rage built up inside of me, I decided I wasn't going to let Ambi or Odin scare me off like they do everyone else. I heard the bell ring in the distance. I cleaned up the blood dripping from my arm and wrapped it in the bandages I had hidden in the middle console. Once I was all wrapped up, I grabbed my backpack and quickly headed back toward the school. I knew I would see Ambi and Odin in my next few classes, but I wasn't going to let them get to me. I would just ignore them and focus on my studies, at least that's what I thought.

Everything went fine when dealing with Ambi, she didn't try to mess with me at all. Odin, on the other hand, didn't make it quite that easy for me. He somehow managed to get my Algebra partner, Christopher, to switch seats with him. Mr. Ferguson wasn't in class and the substitute didn't realize we had assigned seats.

"Why are you sitting here Odin?" I asked, frustrated with him.

"I want to talk to you Lilith." The substitute had us work on a worksheet and I tried my best to just ignore

Odin, but found it very difficult since every time I looked up, he would be staring at me with a smile on his face. It wasn't a creepy smile though it was more like an apologetic smile, like he was begging for my forgiveness. It was becoming hard for me to concentrate on my worksheet when all I could think about how close he was to me.

I dreamt of the day when Odin Edgerson would notice me but not like this. This never happened in my daydreams or any of my dreams for that matter. Him watching me for almost a whole class period became very awkward. Being fed up with the way he was beginning to make me feel, I finally asked, "Odin could you please stop staring at me?"

"I'm sorry Lilith. I'm not trying to be weird but there is just something about you today that makes it kind of hard to take my eyes off of you."

"Oh, you mean like every day before when you never even noticed me and now all of a sudden today, I can't get you to leave me alone? Please Odin. You never even spoke to me before today, why now?" Sometimes I could just smack myself in the face. I have this thing missing in my DNA called a mouth filter and I tend to say what's on my mind before thinking about it. And this is one of those moments.

Before he could respond, the bell rang letting us know school was over for the day. I gathered my things and headed for my car. I fumbled through my backpack trying to find my keys when I heard someone shaking them behind me. Aggravation filled me as I turned around and noticed Odin standing there holding my keys in the air. "How did you get those?"

"You dropped them," he said, as I tried to jerk them from his hand, but he was much quicker and taller than me. Before handing me the keys he said, "Look, I think we got off on the wrong foot. I would like to start over with you. Would you like to grab something to eat with me? I will explain everything to you."

Reluctantly, I agreed but suggested we take separate cars. I don't trust Odin enough to be in a car alone with him. I only agreed to join him because I wanted answers. I needed the answers. I needed to know why they have been watching me.

About the Author

Jessica lives in Maine with her husband and three children. She started writing poetry when she was 10 years old. She has been published in several Poetry Society books. She has won the Publisher's Choice Award for her poem A Lost Soul. She has always had a passion for reading which is what led to her becoming an author. Corruption of the Heart was her debut series under the pen name Jessica Manson.

Also By the Author

Jessica Manson

<u>The Corruption Series</u>

<u>Corruption of the Heart</u>

<u>Beautiful Corruption</u>

<u>Eternal Corruption</u>

J. L. Booth

Shattered Promises

About the Publisher

Kingston Publishing Company, founded by C. K. Green, is dedicated to providing authors an affordable way to turn their dream into a reality. We publish over 100+ titles annually in multiple formats including print and ebook across all major platforms.

We offer every service you will ever need to take an idea and publish a story. We are here to help authors make it in the industry. We want to provide a positive experience that will keep you coming back to us. Whether you want a traditional publisher who offers all the amenities a publishing company should or an author who prefers to self-publish, but needs additional help – we are here for you.

Now Accepting Manuscripts!
Please send query letter and manuscript to:
submissions@kingstonpublishing.com
Visit our website at www.kingstonpublishing.com